CIVILIZATIONAL EVOLUTION

Awareness Principle in Basic Instincts

Bayu Jatmiko

ISBN: 9798859005611
Imprint: Independently published

Cover design by: Canva

Foreword

This book has been translated from Indonesian to English with the assistance of AI ChatGPT 3.5 from the author's own book titled "Mortido : Ketakutan, Keserakahan dan Keawasan Sebuah Evolusi Peradaban," which was published in 2018. This book has undergone changes in the form of more comprehensive theoretical development but without altering the overall content. The following are endorsement words from the book "Mortido, second edition" published in 2020, by Dr. Juneman Abraham, S.Psi, who obtained the title of Professor in the field of Social Psychology in 2023.

"I have read the theme of Psychology of Death covered in various works, ranging from its rational psychology (e.g. Louis Leahy) to its empirical psychology - represented by the terror management theory (Greenberg, Solomon, and Pyszczynski).

Bayu Jatmiko, a Psychology graduate from Mercu Buana University in Jakarta, has provided a distinctive contribution to this Psychology by laying the foundation that there is a paradoxical principle within the unconscious (with the locus of the death instinct in Classical Psychoanalysis), which is Awareness.

This principle truly possesses the capacity to grow, adapt, and strengthen, advocating for life, albeit vulnerable to being disturbed and suppressed by the voracious desires of various political, economic, educational, and belief systems.

The vulnerability and strength of Awareness, analyzed by Bayu through a bio-psychoanalytic-spiritual approach, demonstrate that the psychological dynamics of death are, as speculated by some, engaging, creative, productive, metamorphic, and capable of refining life.

However, congratulations to Bayu for his efforts:

some of these speculations have now been clarified. Bayu reaffirms a Sufistic invitation - now psychological: Let us die before we die. We are challenged to develop personal to political will to embrace this call!"

Prof. Dr. Juneman Abraham, S.Psi.
Social psychologist, Bina Nusantara University.

Fear

Fear is not a part of human nature.
Fear is a disturbance of thought and not something normal.
Fear is learned.

Fear is something normal.
Fear is something usual.
Fear exists within every human being.
The three statements above have mostly been accepted
as truths. They are more widely accepted than the truth
about the existence of God, which is still debated.
The three statements above are incorrect, and this
represents a form of mental revolution.

Fear is not something normal.
Fear is something abnormal.

Fear does not exist within every human being
before being introduced by others.

CONTENTS

Introduction

The civilization of humanity on this Earth continues to show alarming signs in its efforts to sustain its existence in the universe. Wars that never cease, added with terrorism, and unrelenting levels of violence, indicate that our civilization has not progressed since the times of pre-Christian kingdoms, which were also adorned with stories of wars.

When the 9/11 terrorist attacks, which brought down the Twin Towers of the World Trade Center in the United States, occurred, I thought the world would change, and national leaders would adopt different policies to reduce violence, terrorism, and war. However, it seems that I was mistaken. Either the leaders of major nations have no intention to change their policies, or they have the intention but lack the ability to do so.

Moreover, human greed seems to be increasing, leading to the destruction of the environment on this planet we call home. There are indications of climate change that can threaten the sustainability of human civilization on Earth. Violence and greed are two forms of human behavior that seem capable of placing human civilization in question.

Therefore, this book will take you on an adventure into the most basic instincts of human beings, using various approaches ranging from psychology through Sigmund Freud's psychoanalysis theory, then delving into biology and neuroscience, and finally concluding with the philosophy of Buddhism.

The results of this exploration will unveil the deepest mysteries of humanity, the basic instincts that unconsciously control our behavior and actions as human beings. Behaviors that will determine the direction of human civilization in the future, whether it can endure and evolve, or produce a civilization increasingly filled with violence and greed that destroys and threatens the very existence of humanity on this Earth...

CHAPTER 1 HUMAN

Human, yes human, you who are reading this book, and I who am writing this book, we are humans. One of the many species of living beings on this planet Earth. Human beings, our very selves, are one of the greatest mysteries of life in our universe, along with the enigmatic puzzle of life surrounding us.

Humans are complex and intricate living beings when observed in their structure. So complex and intricate that they are capable of questioning the universe, life, creation, and the ultimate question among all questions, "Who am I?" Yes, a question about oneself that perhaps only beings of the human species can ask (perhaps someday in the future, we may interpret the language of monkeys and find that monkeys also ask themselves, "Who am I?").

When humans start to ask, "Who am I?" we, humans, call it a philosophical question, and it can be said that we have begun to philosophize—one of the oldest sciences in the world and considered the mother of all knowledge. Contemplation is the earliest way for humans to attempt to answer all the mysteries in the world, to the extent that it led to the creation of a sculpture representing a great philosopher who once lived on this Earth, the statue of Plato deep in contemplation.

The contemplation of human beings has resulted in various works of thought that we call knowledge. Human contemplation about the mysteries of life and oneself has contributed to the development of human civilization, starting from contemplating the natural phenomena that occur around living human beings, to various knowledge that facilitates human activities.

The earliest ability that helped humans in their activities is language, which is possessed by every living being in its own way. However, human language is one of the most complex compared to other living beings, with its closest competitor being the complex language of whales, which are not actually fish but belong to the mammalian category.

The development of language into writing took a long time, starting from the evolution of ancient humans to modern humans, namely the emergence of Homo sapiens about 200,000 years ago, until the beginning of civilization with the existence of writing about 5000 years before the Common Era.

The transition from language to writing requires a very long process. Before becoming writing, humans first understood symbols or signs or marked things to facilitate their activities. In fact, writing itself is a more complex form of symbols. Writing is one of the achievements of the evolution of civilization.

The use of symbols or markers is not exclusive to humans. Other complex living beings also create symbols or markers, such as dogs marking their territories by urinating in specific locations to inform other dogs of their territory. Symbols have been a part of human life since prehistoric times to the modern era, and through incredible human contemplation, the extraordinary science of symbols was born: mathematics, the universal language for all human civilizations.

In the early stages of civilization, symbols were used to mark territories or power, usually represented in the form of animals with dominating qualities or symbolizing strength. They could also take the form of large trees or natural elements such as mountains or seas. Then, symbols evolved into representations of the sun, moon, and even further into constellations. Symbols also opened the path to the evolution of civilization, leading to art that initially served as symbols of power, but later transformed into a form of worship, laying the foundation for the creation of writing.

Additionally, the use of symbols was related to cardinal

directions and seasons, where both of these aspects helped humans predict the future, especially concerning their need for food and shelter. Understanding cardinal directions and seasons, symbolized by symbols, propelled humanity into mapping, calendars, and astronomy, where humans used the positions of stars to determine directions and seasonal changes.

There were times when human civilizations attached great importance to the knowledge of calendars and astronomy, honoring those who possessed this knowledge, often referred to as "the wise" or, in contemporary terms, religious leaders, shamans, or spiritual experts, whose task was to interpret the astronomical calendar.

During that era, not everyone was capable of reading the calendar, and only certain individuals had this ability to assist their communities. The calendar was used to predict natural phenomena such as seasons and weather, which were related to agriculture, or natural disasters such as droughts and floods, by predicting the arrival of summer, rainy season, and winter.

The importance of the calendar during that time led various civilizations around the world to construct buildings as symbols and pride in the calendars they possessed, such as the construction of pyramids in Egypt, which were related to the positions of stars[1], The highly detailed Maya calendar[2] and the arrangement of stones in Stonehenge in England, which is related to astronomy[3] Mount Padang in Cianjur, Indonesia, may also have a connection to the field of astronomy with its own understanding of calendars. As human understanding of mapping, astronomy, and calendars developed, knowledge in other fields also increased, such as Mathematics and Natural Sciences. Eventually, writing emerged, initially in the form of symbols or pictures, and later, alphabets were created through human intellectual efforts, marking the departure from prehistoric times.

The invention of writing significantly advanced human thinking through contemplation. Initially, human contemplation revolved around the forces of nature that affected human life. Natural phenomena, not yet comprehensible through logical contemplation, led humans to create symbols representing powerful entities that caused these phenomena, which were referred to as gods.

These gods were associated with various natural elements such as fire, water, wind, and others. Not only did humans contemplate gods, but they also developed the understanding of a single God or monotheism. Monotheism likely emerged due to conflicts between civilizations, leading to the dominance of a victorious god or through the profound contemplation of a single, all-powerful God who governs everything.

Various gods and the understanding of God, along with the development of writing and artistic works, gave rise to distinctive cultures in civilizations like Egypt, Greece, India, China, and others. As gods were worshipped and revered in relation to natural phenomena, human contemplation also led to reflections on humanity itself, involving moral, ethical, and truth-related thoughts, marking the rapid development of Philosophy across the world.

People began learning and contemplating about themselves, posing questions like "Who am I?", "Why was I created?", "Who created me?", "Why do I suffer?", "What happens after death?", "How does life work?", and other philosophical questions. The ancient Greek philosophers, such as Aristotle, Socrates, and Plato, along with other philosophers from Greece, China (Taoism and Confucianism), India (Hinduism and Buddhism), contributed to these contemplations.

The contemplation and understanding of God brought a notable difference between monotheism and polytheism, especially in governing societies. The role of a single God not only replaced the polytheistic gods in controlling natural phenomena but also became a spiritual philosophical understanding of the relationship between humanity and the Creator.

This single God, with complex rules for its followers,

formed its own structure within societies, which we call Religion. Meanwhile, the simpler gods, based on natural phenomena, gradually faded away, replaced by monotheistic religions. However, the gods, while no longer governing life, still influenced religious structures, as seen in Hinduism with its diverse sects.

In India, Buddha's teachings shifted into a religion, although more focused on wisdom regarding human life, represented by Buddha himself as an enlightened being. Following the era of ancient Greek philosophy, human contemplation revolved more around religion, while philosophy began developing into specialized sciences that practically helped human daily life, such as Medicine, Mathematics, Chemistry, Physics, and other scientific fields.

During the religious era, human contemplation often revolved around oneself, their relationship with God, and fellow humans. Themes of contemplation often centered on life after death, heaven and hell, and divine commands and prohibitions, along with their punishments, including sins. Religious philosophical thinking flourished in Europe with the spread of Catholicism and in the Middle East with the spread of Islam.

In India, Hinduism and Buddhism continued to develop, as did Taoism and Confucianism in China. Each of these philosophical teachings focused on understanding oneself and the surrounding environment. Eventually, the teachings of Hinduism and Buddhism reached Indonesia.

After the religious era, the pursuit of understanding human nature delved deeper into scientific fields, separate from philosophy, which had given birth to various branches of knowledge. Starting from the Renaissance, known as the Enlightenment era in Europe, humans desired to express themselves artistically after being suppressed under the power of the church for so long.

The resurgence of art was followed by the resurgence of other scientific disciplines, as the "truth" of knowledge was previously controlled by the church. This resurgence also encompassed the desire to learn more about oneself, eventually giving rise to Psychology as a distinct scientific field.

With the birth of Psychology, humans specifically studied human behavior, aiming to understand human behavior itself. The hope was that a better understanding of human psychology would directly lead to improved human life and, indirectly, to a more advanced human civilization.

Despite studying various aspects of human beings, such as Philosophy, Psychology, and Biological Sciences, including Neurosciences, we have not yet fully understood ourselves, and human behavior has shown minimal significant changes since the early days of civilization, from the ancient Egyptian and contemporary civilizations.

Violence and wars still dominate human behavior and conduct in civilization. The issues of welfare and economic disparities remain pressing problems for humanity, with no apparent solutions in sight. This includes the environmental damage caused by human behavior in the industrial sector, leading to global warming.

Even the renowned physicist Stephen Hawking revised his previous prediction that the Earth could sustain human life for 1000 more years, reducing it to 100 years. He urged humans to find another planet to replace Earth, which might no longer be inhabitable due to various problems, such as climate change, endemic diseases, overpopulation, and potential asteroid impacts[4].

Human behavior can be said to have not undergone significant changes from the era of kingdoms to the modern age. If the measure is based on human values, it could even be argued that the level of human civilization has experienced regression due to the threat of extinction caused by human behavior itself. Especially economic greed, which gives rise to violence and wars in various parts of the world, ranging from small-scale unhealthy competition in businesses to unending wars, both open conflicts and terrorism.

Economic greed leads to environmental degradation, and

it is uncertain how long the Earth can withstand the pace of destruction caused by human civilization before it becomes uninhabitable. Greed is undoubtedly one of the behaviors that need to be studied and researched as an effort to better understand oneself, a topic that seems not to have been fully comprehended by various humanities disciplines existing today.

The unchanged behavior of humans from the beginning of history to the modern era, and the tendency of the human civilization's condition to worsen, calls for a change. **Psychology** is one of the leading sciences responsible for providing solutions to improve human behavior on an individual level and for humanity as a whole. One of the essential branches of psychology is psychoanalysis, pioneered by Sigmund Freud.

Freud's theories have significantly influenced contemporary human civilization, particularly his theory of libido with its principle of pleasure rooted in the subconscious. The theory of libido, which emphasizes pleasure or satisfaction, is widely utilized by economic actors in their marketing strategies to trigger the subconscious pleasure principle of consumers. Apart from the theory of libido, Freud laid the foundation for the structure of human personality.

The basis of human personality structure, as developed by Freud, was further explored and developed by his student, Carl Gustav Jung, who eventually diverged from Freud's ideas. Jung, in developing his own personality structure from Freud's foundation, discovered vast opportunities for exploration, aimed at helping individuals understand themselves better. Ultimately, this understanding could lead to changes in human behavior, making it more humane and compassionate on a general and comprehensive level within human civilization.

In the next chapter, we will explore the deepest and most primitive instincts within humans to unravel the mystery of human nature itself.

CHAPTER 2
PSYCHOANALYSIS, ID, AND MORTIDO

Psychoanalysis or depth psychology is one of the branches of psychology founded by one of the world's renowned figures, Sigmund Freud. Within psychoanalysis, there are still many theories that can be developed and refined in line with the advancements of time. The development of biological and medical theories can be utilized to perfect psychoanalysis.

The theories within psychoanalysis leave ample room for imagination to play and develop these theories to become more complete, especially in predicting not only individual human behavior but also controlling or influencing the masses, a concept that had never been thought of before. This is because there are still gaps in psychoanalytic theories, waiting to be filled to unveil the mysteries of psychoanalysis inherited from Sigmund Freud and his colleagues. Psychoanalysis is one of the branches of psychology that studies human behavior by analyzing what the individual thinks, including their ideals, perceptions, imagination, and memories. In the theory of psychoanalysis, Sigmund Freud developed a theory of personality, stating that human personality consists of three systems: id, superego, and ego. Superego is the place of moral ethics and various cognitive considerations about right and wrong.

Picture 1 Personality Structure

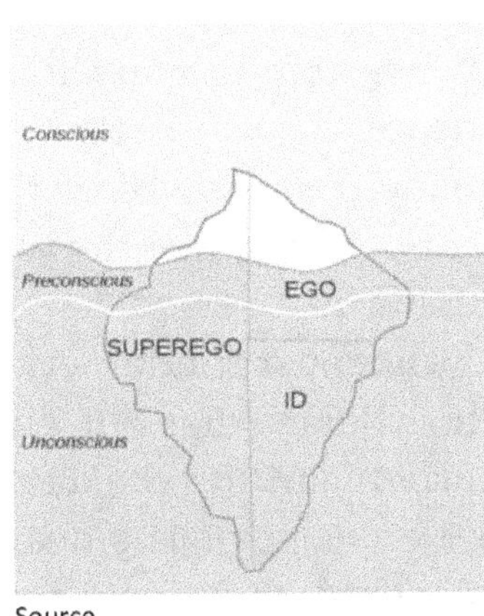

Source https://commons.wikimedia.org/wiki/File:Structural-Iceberg.svg

The id is the place of primitive instincts, which are instincts that have not been shaped or influenced by culture. These instincts include the life instinct, which drives the desire to live and preserve life, and the death instinct, which drives the desire for death. The ego acts as the meeting point of the superego and the id, with the task of channeling the id's instincts, adjusted by the superego, into the conscious mind or suppressing id's instincts if they conflict with the superego, keeping them in the unconscious mind.

Based on the explanation above, we now understand the structure of the psychoanalytic personality, which consists of the ego, superego, and id. From the diagram above, we can see that only a small part of our personality is conscious or above the surface of the water, while all the thoughts and instincts that we are not aware of reside in the unconscious, beneath the surface of the water, comprising the majority of our personality structure.

This indicates that humans perform many actions automatically or without full control. As a consequence, there are more actions that emerge automatically without conscious command compared to actions or thoughts that we consciously initiate.

The id, as the source of basic instincts, is the origin of human desires to stay alive and fulfill the basic needs necessary for life. Therefore, throughout this book, we will focus more on this id instinct, delving into the deepest and most primitive part of the human psychological structure.

Sigmund Freud divided the id into two drives: the life drive and the death drive. The life drive refers to the sexual drive or libido, while the death drive represents aggression, which leads people to attack others, fight, wage wars, or experience anger, with the ultimate goal being death.

Freud believed that all humans, in their unconscious, possess a desire for death, but this death drive is strongly suppressed by the instinct for life. The principle followed by the id is the pleasure principle, which means that the goal of the id is to satisfy all these primitive instincts.

From the explanation about the id, the most fundamental aspect to perfect the psychoanalytic theory lies in the foundation of the theory itself, particularly regarding the death drive. Freud did not actually intend the concept of the death drive to include instincts, and he considered these instincts unimportant for the life of living beings, as they go against nature and contradict the intuitive drive for life[5].

The impulse for death began to emerge when Freud analyzed the traumas experienced by soldiers in World War I. In his observations, Freud found that patients kept reliving their traumatic war experiences in their dreams, which contradicted his understanding that the id should be governed by the pleasure principle.

Then, Freud discovered that in children's games, especially in hide-and-seek between a child and their mother, there was a tense condition due to the loss of the mother that was constantly repeated in the game. This hide-and-seek game situation made Freud struggle to connect the loss of the mother with the pleasure principle, as losing one's mother is a stressful experience for a child.

The next condition arose when Freud found patients with compulsive behavior who kept repeating painful experiences or incorporating them into their own lives repeatedly. Freud was perplexed because the patients could not leave their past traumatic experiences as part of their memories. These painful compulsive conditions originated from the unconscious, once again contradicting the id's pleasure principle.

Upon observing these conditions, Freud cautiously made assumptions, which were still speculative in his view, that there exists an impulse for death within humans. He believed that this impulse originated from the earliest stages of living beings, where there was a desire to return to an inanimate state, and thus, in the primitive unconscious, the desire to return to inanimate objects still exists[6].

In the further development of psychoanalytic theory, the "death instinct" did not receive the same prominence as the "life instinct" that represents the libido with its pleasure principle within the id. Freud's developmental theory was based on the pleasure principle, representing the "life instinct," while the "death instinct" was marginalized and less developed.

From the beginning, Freud emphasized that the "death instinct" was still an assumption, indicating his dissatisfaction with this aspect of the theory. Therefore, the "death instinct" remains a part of the id that can be further explored.

We often hear the use of the term "libido." One example of its use is by a public figure, former Minister of Social Affairs in President Joko Widodo's cabinet during the 2014-2018 period, Khofifah Indar Parawansa. She suggested measures to deal with sexual offenders by administering certain chemicals that could paralyze their libido[7]. Regarding the nerve of libido itself, it is not yet fully understood, but biologically, libido is closely related to sexual hormones such as testosterone and estrogen.

Initially introduced by Freud as the life instinct in the id or the subconscious, the term libido was initially more closely associated with the field of psychology than biology, despite Freud himself being a medical doctor. However, the term libido generally refers to sexual desire, and it has been widely used in various fields such as biology, social sciences, and psychology by the general public.

The counterpart of the life instinct or libido, the death instinct, is not as popularly used as the term libido. Freud's followers have tried to find a suitable term to accompany libido, some proposed "destrudo," while others used "mortido." I will use the term "mortido" to represent the death instinct alongside libido, representing the life instinct.

The term "mortido" was first introduced by Paul Federn, one of Freud's disciples[8]. However, the fate of mortido or other terms like destrudo is not like libido, which has already been widely used by the public. The use of the term mortido is rare, and many people do not understand its meaning. Freud himself did not consider the death instinct essential for life and believed it to be strongly suppressed by the life instinct.

In the subsequent development of psychoanalytic theory by Freud, more emphasis was placed on developing the theory of libido and its symbols in dreams. Freud also developed the theory of development based on the pleasure principle, which had a stronger connection with libido than mortido.

The death instinct seems to be nothing more than an assumption used to patch up the holes in Freud's pleasure principle theory. As a patch, this assumption was not developed into a strong enough theory that could be embraced by the general public, similar to the theory of libido.

The representation of the death instinct by mortido remains a mystery that has not been solved, not developed, or perhaps intentionally left undeveloped or even kept secret within the broader scope of the famous psychoanalytic theory. Even more intriguing is the fact that the death instinct resides in the id, which forms the foundation of this theory. Therefore, any change in the understanding of the death instinct would significantly impact the theory of personality within psychoanalysis.

The mystery of mortido will be explored through three approaches: the psychoanalytic approach, followed by the biological approach, and finally the spiritual approach. Psychology has a close connection with biology, while the spiritual approach is used to unveil the mysteries and secrets surrounding the spiritual world, allowing for spiritual understanding to be studied scientifically or at least rationally, without relying solely on beliefs or faith.

First, we will delve into the psychoanalytic approach. The essence of psychoanalytic theory lies in its structure of personality, namely the superego, ego, and id. In the earlier chapters, we briefly outlined the basics of psychoanalysis, and now we will deepen our understanding of it.

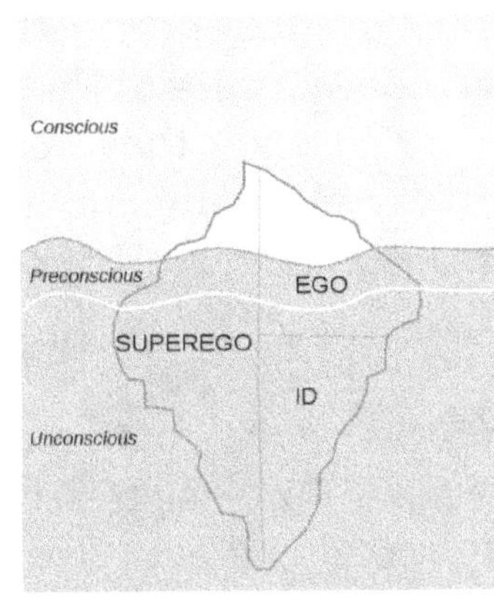

Picture 1 Personality Structure

Source
https://commons.wikimedia.org/wiki/Fil
e:Structural-Iceberg.svg

I will take the explanation of the personality structure from the book by Mr. Sarlito W. Sarwono [9]. The need to understand the personality structure first is to comprehend the position of the mortido secret within the personality structure and its influence on the entire personality. Alright, here is Mr. Sarlito's explanation from the book *"berkenalan dengan aliran-aliran dan tokoh psikologi"* regarding the personality structure based on psychoanalytic theory, which of course, his explanation is much better than if I were to explain it

Psychoanalysis

Sigmund Freud explained the structure of personality as an iceberg. The part that appears above the water surface is the smallest part, the peak of the iceberg, which in the realm of the mind is called the consciousness. Slightly below the water surface is the part he called the preconsciousness. The content of the preconsciousness is things that can come to consciousness at any time. The largest part of the iceberg is beneath the water surface and in the realm of the mind, it represents the unconsciousness. This unconsciousness contains impulses that want to emerge to the surface or to consciousness. These impulses continuously press upwards, while the space above is very limited. The "ego" (the self) remains, which becomes the center of consciousness and has to regulate which impulses should stay in the unconsciousness. Most of the impulses that originate from the unconsciousness must indeed remain there, but they are not dormant; instead, they keep pressing, and if the "ego" is not strong enough to restrain these pressures, mental disturbances may occur.

The impulses found in the unconsciousness are partly those that exist from birth, namely sexual and aggressive impulses, and partly they stem from past experiences that once happened at the conscious level and were traumatic, so they need to be repressed and placed into the unconsciousness. According to Freud, all human behavior originates from these impulses located deep within the unconsciousness. Freud's structure of personality, consisting of consciousness, preconsciousness, and unconsciousness, can be likened to a building where there are three systems interacting: the superego, the ego, and the id. As mentioned before, the id contains primitive impulses, namely the impulses for life and the impulses for death, which will be our main focus. The purpose of the id is to satisfy all these primitive impulses.

The superego, on the other hand, is the opposite of the id. This system is entirely formed by culture. When a child is young, they receive education from their parents, and through this education, they learn what is good, what is bad, what is allowed, and what is prohibited, what aligns with societal norms and what violates them. As the child grows into an adult, all the norms acquired through education become the content of the superego, so the superego contains impulses to do good, impulses to follow societal norms, and so on. The impulses or energy originating from the superego will attempt to suppress the impulses arising from the id because the primitive impulses from the id may not be acceptable or compatible with the superego. This is where the conflict between the impulses from the id and the superego occurs. Sometimes the superego wins, and sometimes the id is stronger[10].

Ego is the system where the two impulses from the id and superego clash. The function of the ego is to maintain a balance between the other two systems, so that not too many impulses from the id are brought into consciousness, and likewise, not all demands from the superego are fulfilled. The ego itself does not possess impulses or energy. It merely operates on the principle of reality (reality principle), which means adjusting the impulses from the id or superego with the realities of the external world. The ego is the only system directly connected to the external world, allowing it to consider these reality factors[11].

That's essentially the structure of personality according to Sigmund Freud. Now, let's focus on the Id, the source of all human behavioral impulses. According to Freud, the Id operates on the principle of gratification or pleasure, represented by the libido. However, this understanding is not agreed upon by Freud's former friend, the renowned Carl Gustav Jung, which led to their parting ways and the development of their own theories.

The difference between Freud and Jung lies in their interpretation of libido. Jung expanded the understanding of libido, not just relating it to sexual satisfaction, but as the energy underlying various mental processes such as thinking, feeling, desiring, sensing, and more. Consequently, the Id contains autonomous impulses, each with its own drive[12].

Jung expanded his understanding of libido and extended the principle of pleasure but did not add another principle that represents one of the mysteries, namely the death instinct. The life instinct represented by libido and the principle of pleasure are so strong that they suppress the death instinct, which could be why Freud overlooked it. However, is this really the case? Is it possible that the id does not only have one principle, namely the pleasure principle, but also has **another principle** that is completely different or even contrary to the pleasure principle? Perhaps it goes beyond just expanding the understanding of the pleasure principle as Jung did, but truly represents a different principle that embodies the death instinct.

Freud assumed that the life instinct strongly suppresses the death instinct, but it remains an assumption that indicates Freud's uncertainty. Let us revisit the theory of libido to unravel this assumption and to explore the possibility of a new way of thinking.

Id (Libido x Mortido)

Libido is the life instinct based on the pleasure principle, and this principle dominates the id. The main motivation of this theory is the human need for reproduction (development) and attraction to the opposite sex for marriage. Additionally, satisfying the needs for pleasure, such as eating, drinking, and finding a comfortable place to live, also becomes a primary drive or motivation in this fundamental theory, solidifying the pleasure principle within the id.

The basic needs for self-preservation, such as eating, drinking, and shelter, serve the purpose of staying alive.

However, these needs differ from the need for development, reproduction or mating, where the latter is used to procreate offspring. Nevertheless, both aspects share the same principle of satisfaction, wherein once these needs are fulfilled, a sense of contentment is experienced.

The basic need for self-preservation is distinct from the need for development. Apart from eating, drinking, and finding shelter or protection, there are other instincts involved, such as the instinct for survival, self-defense against danger, or the instinct to protect oneself and one's offspring, particularly in the context of humans, where it includes the parental instinct to protect their children.

The survival instinct does not yield satisfaction or pleasure like sexual instincts; in fact, humans may need to display aggression to defend themselves, which can be considered part of the death instinct, as it involves aggressive behavior. Within the need for self-preservation, there are two aspects: the instinct to live, which includes eating, drinking, and seeking shelter, and the instinct to die, manifested in aggressive actions taken to protect oneself from danger. It should be noted that the death instinct also includes the aggressive impulse to harm oneself, as discussed by Freud.

The life instinct encompasses the need for development and some basic self-preservation needs, while the death instinct encompasses some of the basic self-preservation needs. The categorization is as follows:

Drives for life :
- **Development needs**
- **Basic Self-Preservation needs (clothing, food, shelter)**
  - **Eating**
  - **Drinking**
  - **Shelter**
  - **Clothing**

Drives for death :

- **Aggressive actions for self-preservation (survival)**
- **Aggressive actions towards self-harm**

As seen above, the death instinct actually encompasses two basic needs: the need to live and another aspect involving aggressive acts of self-harm leading towards an individual's death. Both of these aspects fall under the death instinct as they involve aggressive behaviors, with one being directed outward and the other directed inward towards oneself.

Although outward aggression is part of the need for survival and can be categorized with eating, drinking, and other self-preservation needs, this aggressive behavior does not represent the principle of satisfaction and thus does not fall under the life instinct, which is based on the pleasure principle.

However, the need for survival also contradicts the death instinct, even in the form of aggressive behavior, because it is motivated by the drive for self-preservation and not the primitive desire to return to an inanimate state, as assumed by Freud. Therefore, the aggressive drive for self-preservation is not a suitable fit for the life instinct as it does not align with the pleasure principle and cannot be classified under the death instinct either, as it aims at survival rather than death.

The next question is where to place this aggressive drive for self-preservation. This drive cannot be eliminated as it is evident that the self-preservation drive in the form of aggression originates from the unconscious and is primitive in nature. All living beings strive to preserve themselves in their own ways and develop adaptive systems necessary for their survival, making it clearly a primitive aspect residing in the id. Interestingly, Freud did not delve into this aspect but remained focused on libido and its pleasures.

Freud did explain defense mechanisms, which are patterns of self-defense developed by the ego when faced with threats or persistent primitive urges that are not allowed to emerge by the superego[13]. The interesting thing about these defense mechanisms is that the patterns developed by Freud are closely related to the aggressive drive for self-preservation and are more prominent compared to the drives originating from libido. The aggressive drive for self-preservation clearly needs to maintain its position in the id since it logically exists in every living being.

The issue regarding the position of the aggressive drive for self-preservation can be elucidated by returning to the fundamental drives. Based on the categorization of the id mentioned earlier, if we first break down the drives for life and the death instinct, we have three basic groups of drives, assuming that the aggressive drive for self-preservation in the form of attack can be combined with other self-preservation needs such as clothing, food, and shelter. Therefore, the division would be as follows:

- **Drive for development**
- **Drive for self-preservation**
    - **Provision of clothing, food, and shelter**
    - **Aggressive action outwardly**
- **Aggressive drive for self-harm**

Analysis based on the basic principles working within the id would be as follows. The drive for development, which fundamentally originates from the reproductive drive, clearly operates based on the principle of pleasure or satisfaction. While the drive for self-preservation has a partial principle of satisfaction and some other principles. On the other hand, the aggressive drive for self-harm clearly lacks any principle of satisfaction because when successfully self-harming and reaching its peak, such as in suicide, the individual cannot possibly feel satisfied as they are already dead. From this, it can be concluded that the id does not solely operate based on the principle of satisfaction but involves **other principles** as well.

The next analysis is whether these drives are primitive instincts in humans, forming the basis of all human behavior. The drive for development is undoubtedly a primitive instinct, as humans and all living beings possess a natural instinct to mate in order to propagate their species, with the aim of preserving their kind.

The drive for self-preservation is also very apparent, as humans and all living beings possess this natural instinct to maintain their existence. In fact, the drive for self-preservation must exist before the drive for development, as individuals cannot possibly engage in reproduction or mating if they do not have the initial desire to self-preservation.

The last drive, the aggressive drive for self-harm, is the most **doubtful** to be situated in the id. According to Freud, humans have a desire to return to a state akin to an inanimate object, leading to the emergence of the death drive. Freud even added that this drive underlies outward aggressive behavior as a form of displacement – deliberately misplacing or confusing the drive, changing it from being directed inward towards the self to being directed outward due to the stronger suppression of the death drive by the life drive. Hence, the death drive that was initially directed towards oneself is redirected outward.

Displacement is one of the defense mechanisms developed by Freud[14]. The aggression drive proposed by Freud is initially preceded by traumatic conditions, compulsive disorders, or depression, where these conditions are caused by an event, a past event preceding them.

For example, in a traumatized person, there is a past event that is very painful, making it impossible for them to forget the trauma and keep remembering it. According to Freud, when there is an unpleasant event in the theory of defense mechanisms, it will be suppressed or repressed into the subconscious mind. Freud was puzzled when he encountered cases where the client kept remembering the trauma as if there was a drive to keep experiencing the pain.

Upon observation, it becomes evident from the above-mentioned traumatic case that the death drive initially originates from a **real** event outside the psychological realm of the client, affecting the client's psychological state. The event external to the individual is what triggers the death drive, not an inherent part of the individual.

This is different from the drive for procreation, where the desire to mate arises from within oneself, and then humans seek a partner. In the case of the self-preservation drive, feelings of hunger emerge from within the individual, as well as feelings of thirst and the need to find a comfortable place to rest, which are drives that arise from within the individual when feeling thirsty, tired, or sleepy.

Next is the self-preservation drive in the form of aggression. This drive emerges when there is a threat from outside the individual and not a threat that enters the individual, such as viruses or bacteria causing illness. In such cases, humans already have their own highly sophisticated immune system that works effectively.

The external threats to the individual include natural disasters such as earthquakes, volcanic eruptions, flash floods, or fires, as well as threats from wild animals like aggressive dogs and other predatory animals. Additionally, threats from other aggressive individuals, such as humans wanting to attack violently or express anger and various aggressive actions, are also considered external threats.

When such threats arise, the self-preservation drive in the form of aggression manifests itself in two choices: fight or flight, based on an assessment of the situation. If the individual feels superior to the threat, such as a small growling cat, they will fight the small cat, causing the cute little cat to run away. Conversely, if the threat is a large cat, the individual will feel inferior and run away frantically.

The self-preservation drive in the form of aggression towards the external self requires a threat from outside the individual, and it does not automatically originate from within the individual, like the drives for procreation, hunger, thirst, or the desire to be lazy or rest.

Apparently, this is similar to the aggression drive towards the internal self, which also requires an external threat first.

However, the crucial similarity here is that we can draw an interesting conclusion when we examine this closely. The aggression drive towards the internal self is preceded by a **past event** that threatens the individual's existence.

It turns out that an event threatening the individual's existence triggers the emergence of the self-preservation drive in the form of aggression towards the external self. If the threat can be eliminated, the aggressive drive will disappear. However, if the threat does not disappear or keeps recurring, it can become an event that causes **psychological trauma** for the individual.

This trauma will be suppressed into the subconscious mind along with the aggressive drive that pursues the threat causing the trauma. In some cases, this trauma often emerges into the conscious mind, resulting in the aggressive drive that harms oneself. From this, it is evident that the drive to harm oneself is initially preceded by the self-preservation drive in the form of aggression towards the external self.

There is a transformation of outward impulses into inward ones due to the presence of trauma that cannot be repressed into the subconscious and outward to the conscious mind, causing the individual's aggressive impulses to also surface in the conscious mind, chasing after that trauma and manifesting as self-harm in the conscious mind. Self-harm occurs because the aggressive drive pursues the threat posed by the aforementioned trauma, which is located in the **individual's memory**.

From this, it appears that the self-preservation instinct in the form of outward aggressive impulses of an individual is actually similar to the self-harming aggressive impulses. Both of these impulses stem from the same source. And the self-harming aggressive impulse is merely an extension of **the self-preservation instinct** in the form of outward aggressive impulses of the individual.

Therefore, the drive to harm oneself can be eliminated and combined with the self-preservation drive in the form of aggression towards the external self, or we can abbreviate it as the aggressive drive for self-preservation. Thus, the current categorization of the id :

- **Drive for procreation**
- **Drive for self-preservation**
  - **Clothing, Food, and Shelter**
  - **Aggressive drive for self-preservation**

CHAPTER 3
AGGRESSIVENESS

Now, we have two drives, namely the drive for procreation and the self-preservation drive, consisting of clothing, food, shelter, and aggressive actions. Meanwhile, the death drive or the aggressive drive in the form of self-harm can be eliminated. The next issue is whether the aggressive self-preservation drive is a primitive drive.

As we know, the aggressive drive only emerges when there is an external threat, which differs from the procreation drive and the drive for clothing, food, and shelter that are inherently active, although they can become stronger with external stimuli. For instance, in individuals who have reached puberty, there is a period of sexual arousal, and when approached or enticed by the opposite sex, the procreation drive becomes stronger. Similarly, in a hungry individual, the aroma of food can intensify the feeling of hunger.

But what about the aggressive self-preservation drive? This drive will not manifest if there is no threat. If an individual never feels threatened throughout their life, this drive will not emerge. Therefore, before categorizing the aggressive self-preservation drive as part of the id or not, it is worthwhile to become acquainted with a Nobel laureate in biology in 1973, Mr. Konrad Lorenz, and his theory of aggression.

Lorenz was an ethologist, a branch of biology specializing in the study of animal behavior. He conducted research on aggression and its basic instincts, particularly in animals.

According to Lorenz, there are four fundamental instincts in animals: the drive for procreation or sexuality, hunger or thirst, the drive to flee or escape, and finally, the aggressive drive to fight. Lorenz referred to them as "the big four" (sexuality, hunger, flight, aggression)[15].

As an instinct, aggression is spontaneous and autonomous. Therefore, this aggressive impulse arises not as a reaction to external factors but as an urge from within the individual that requires outward expression. This is different from the aggression drive expressed by Freud, known as the death instinct.

The theory developed by Lorenz reveals four drives: sexuality, hunger, flight, and aggression. The sexuality drive is similar to Freud's and does not need further elaboration. Hunger can be assumed and combined with the need for self-preservation, including clothing, food, and shelter. The aggression drive becomes the central topic of our discussion, and we will also explore another drive called flight, which pertains to the impulse of self-preservation and how it can emerge.

One interesting aspect shared by both Freud and Lorenz is their view on the aggressive drive. Although they have different opinions on the direction of this aggression, where Freud believes it is directed inwards towards self-harm, and if it is directed outwards, it is called displacement, which is one form of defense mechanism; while Lorenz's aggressive drive is directed outward to harm others or for self-protection. However, both of them agree that aggression is a natural instinct or impulse that exists inherently, and without needing external stimuli or causes, this drive always exists and requires expression.

The subsequent explanation will help us understand whether this aggressive drive truly exists within individuals and always requires expression, like sexual needs or basic self-preservation needs such as clothing, food, and shelter, or if it needs specific stimuli such as threats or other forms.

Flight and Aggression, these two drives arise from the same state of being threatened experienced by both animals and humans, and this is already evident. Next, we will investigate whether this aggressive drive is an instinct or a lasting trait that requires expression or if it is only a response to specific stimuli.

A physiological figure who specifically studies this is Walter Bradford Cannon; he does not study other drives such as sexual needs or basic self-preservation needs. Rather, he focuses on what he calls the "flight or fight" response in an organism[16].

Flight or fight is a response to stressful or dangerous situations that threaten an individual. In this context, Cannon conducted research on animals, where the response given by the animals is related to the sympathetic nervous system, which involves an increase in heart rate and blood pressure, providing more oxygen and glucose to the muscles.

Furthermore, aggression or aggressive behavior has many theories. The explanations provided by the aforementioned figures are approaches that suggest aggression is innate or based on instinct. However, there are other theories stating that aggressive behavior is a reaction to stimuli present in the environment.

Dollar et al. (1933) and Miller (1941) propose that aggression is triggered by frustration, which occurs when there are obstacles to achieving a goal. Thus, aggression becomes an outlet for the feelings of frustration[17]. In further developments, according to Berkowitz (1978, 1989), it is stated that frustration that leads to anger is what can trigger aggression, and not all frustrations can result in feelings of anger [18]. Frustration that leads to aggression is also caused by the gap between expectations and reality, causing the individual to feel deprived, as mentioned by Berkowitz [19].

Meanwhile, Myers (1966) divided aggression into two types: hostile or emotional aggression and instrumental aggression, which is aggression as a means to achieve other goals [20]. Moyer (1968) presented a classification of seven forms of aggression from a biological and evolutionary perspective, namely[21].

1. Predatory Aggression: Attack on prey by a predator.
2. Inter-male Aggression: Competition between males of the same species for access to specific resources such as females, dominance, status, etc.
3. Fear-induced Aggression: Aggression associated with efforts to avoid threats.
4. Territorial Aggression: Defending a territorial area from intruders.
5. Maternal Aggression: Aggression from females/ mothers to protect their offspring from threats. There is also paternal aggression.
6. Instrumental Aggression: Aggression aimed at achieving a goal. This aggression is considered a learned response to a particular situation.

Based on the explanation above, there are indeed many other theories of aggression, and further exploration would lead to even broader aspects, not only limited to frustration theory but also including social learning theory regarding the causes of aggression and factors influencing it, such as the social environment, education, parenting, media (TV, internet, pornography), and more.

Nevertheless, the general explanation of the theory of aggressive drive is that it is a response to a stimulus, and the stimuli can vary. Certain biological mechanisms react to these stimuli, resulting in the emergence of aggressive tendencies. However, whether aggression can arise without a stimulus or if biological mechanisms can trigger aggression automatically without **external stimuli** remains a subject of long debate.

Nevertheless, most experts agree, based on the various theories discussed above, that aggressive drive is a response to specific stimuli, which can be threats, competition, or even instrumental means to achieve particular goals, like warfare.

Aggression can be associated with emotions or occur without emotional attachment.

To better understand the aggression drive, let's take a step back and investigate or comprehend the processes within individuals before aggression emerges. This approach will also help us gain a deeper understanding of the wide range of theories surrounding aggression, which spans various fields of study, including biology, cognition, social environment, emotions, heredity, and instincts.

The current approach is vast, and each approach could branch out further. Thus, let's downgrade it by focusing on a biological perspective, which allows for direct and objective examination. Afterward, we can elevate it to the realm of psychology and attempt to elucidate the above-mentioned theories of aggression based on simpler yet more effective theories.

Flight or Fight

To investigate this, we need to go back to Cannon's theory of fight or flight response. Before an individual decides to fight or flee, they will assess the threat they encounter. The individual will consider whether they can confront the threat or if they need to run away from it.

If the threat is a natural disaster, for example, the individual must flee to find a safe place. If the threat is another individual, they will evaluate whether they can handle that person or not. For instance, when facing an angry cat, a human might easily shoo it away with a sudden startling movement, causing the cat to run away clumsily. It might look amusing if the cat slips and falls into a drain, although animal lovers would not appreciate this.

However, the scenario changes when encountering larger cats like tigers, lions, or leopards. In such cases, the individual will undoubtedly decide to flee or save themselves. They might suddenly run or move cautiously, searching for the right moment to escape or finding other ways to save themselves.

Threats are not only related to personal safety. They can also involve the principle of pleasure related to libido, such as being threatened with not getting tasty food or not having an attractive partner. For instance, when an elementary school student is enjoying their snacks, suddenly a middle school student comes and asks for all their snacks or, in other words, snatches their snacks. Since the bully is bigger, the elementary student gives their snacks. However, if the opponent is another jealous child, they might not be given anything, or if the child insists, they might be scolded or given only a portion or all of the snacks, depending on the elementary student's choice.

There can also be threats in the form of competition for a mate, which in some mammals can involve fights as mentioned by Moyer, aggression between males[22]. If the competitor is perceived as evenly matched, they are invited to fight, but if the opponent is seen as stronger, one would prefer to avoid or flee.

The decision to flee or fight in an individual is based on feelings of inferiority or superiority. Feelings of inferiority arise when **the perceived** threat is stronger and more dangerous than oneself. For example, in the case mentioned earlier, facing a tiger that can endanger one's life, a natural disaster that clearly threatens one's safety, or a snack thief with a larger body.

On the other hand, feelings of superiority arise when **the perceived** threat is weaker than oneself. For example, in the case mentioned earlier, facing a cat as a human, so when the human makes a sudden move towards the growling cat, the cat flees in disarray. However, the human might have feelings of inferiority towards the cat, so when a cat just passes by, the human is surprised and startled, and the cat also flees in disarray. Such reactions occur because the human has a perception of inferiority towards cats due to past trauma, such as being scratched by a cat when they were a child.

Traumatic events can change one's perception of threats from superior to inferior and vice versa. For instance, certain experiences and training can change one's perception from inferior to superior, such as in the case of animal handlers dealing with wild animals like tigers, lions, or leopards. Further explanations of how traumatic events can change perceptions of inferiority and superiority will be discussed in subsequent chapters.

Before an individual makes the decision to fight or flee in the face of a threat, the individual undergoes various internal conditions such as fear, anger, or vigilance. According to Cannon, during the fight or flight process, the sympathetic nervous system is activated, which is associated with increased heart rate and blood pressure, providing more oxygen and glucose to important muscles, dilating pupils, and increasing adrenaline. All of these functions help prepare the individual to take action, whether it be to fight or flee. The individual will be in a tense condition, and all senses will try to capture as much information as possible from the surrounding environment. This function is to determine the appropriate action to take in the face of the perceived threat, which is called the state of **vigilance**.

To be vigilant, the individual's brain must quickly coordinate all the information to assess the current situation, reinforced by experiences and knowledge acquired when facing threats. However, there are also conditions where excessive tension can cause an individual to lose their ability to think. In such cases, the brain fails to coordinate all the information received through the senses with the experiences and knowledge possessed. When that happens, the condition experienced by the individual is called **fear** when the threat is perceived as superior to oneself, and **anger** when the threat is perceived as inferior.

Interestingly, before an individual decides to fight or flee in the face of a threat, the individual may experience various conditions within themselves, such as fear, anger, or vigilance. A simple conclusion is that vigilance enables an individual to think quickly in facing threats, while fear or anger causes the individual to lose the ability to think logically when facing threats. Fear clearly makes an individual choose to flee from the threat, while anger makes an individual choose to confront the threat.

As for vigilance, the individual may choose to flee or fight. It is possible that an individual remains vigilant while fleeing, for example, when facing a natural disaster like a volcanic eruption, the individual, in a state of vigilance, tries to flee and think clearly to find a safe path. However, in certain situations, excessively high fear can make an individual lose the ability to flee, such as being so afraid that they faint, become paralyzed, or unable to move, or even urinate. Such situations are not desirable.

On the other hand, being vigilant while confronting a threat can be exemplified when facing someone bothering our partner; we confront them, but not with blind anger or jealousy, we can approach them politely and calmly address the situation, even if they have been bothering or teasing our partner. It won't be effective if we act in blind jealousy, which can lead to unwanted consequences.

Another conclusion is that an individual may have two feelings simultaneously, a combination of fear and vigilance, or a combination of anger and vigilance. The action taken will depend on which feeling is stronger; if fear is stronger, the behavior will reflect fear with vigilance, and vice versa, if vigilance is stronger, the behavior will appear vigilant with an underlying fear.

The same applies to anger and vigilance. From the two simple examples above, we can observe that both the "fight" and "flight" responses can be accompanied by a vigilant attitude, without necessarily involving anger or fear. There are indeed various conclusions regarding vigilance, fear, and anger.

Therefore, we will return to a more fundamental approach based on biology to further understand the mechanisms of "fight" and "flight" in relation to fear, anger, and vigilance. We will revisit the more fundamental approach using

Walter Cannon's theory, who previously introduced the term "fight or flight." This time, we will delve deeper into the concept of **homeostasis**, introduced by Cannon, which is a system that works to maintain the balance of various bodily functions to keep them in equilibrium[23].

CHAPTER 4
HOMEOSTASIS

Homeostasis refers to the resilience or mechanism of maintaining a constant dynamic equilibrium in the internal environment (body of an organism). The term homeostasis pertains to the overall maintenance of resilience within the body. Homeostasis stabilizes the body by regulating the internal environment. This is necessary for the body to function properly. The homeostatic process is crucial for the self-preservation of every cell system, tissue, and body.

Homeostasis in a general sense refers to stability, balance, or equilibrium. Maintaining a stable internal environment requires constant **monitoring**, primarily by the brain and nervous system. The brain receives information from the body and responds appropriately by releasing various substances such as neurotransmitters, catecholamines, and hormones.

Further, the physiology of individual organs facilitates the maintenance of overall body homeostasis. For instance, in the regulation of blood pressure, the release of renin by the kidneys allows blood pressure to remain stable (Renin, Angiotensinogen Protein, Aldosterone System), even though the brain assists in regulating blood pressure through pituitary hormones by releasing Anti-diuretic Hormone (ADH). Thus, homeostasis is maintained throughout the body as a whole, depending on its various components[24].

From the explanation above, it is known that the body always strives to maintain its internal conditions in **a stable**

and balanced state to sustain the self-preservation of every cell, which influences the life of the complex organism as a whole. This ultimately serves the purpose of maintaining the preservation of the organism itself. Generally, homeostasis is useful for maintaining the balance of temperature, pH value, light, humidity, topography, and climate. The part in the brain responsible for maintaining this homeostatic balance is the hypothalamus.

The hypothalamus is a part of the brain composed of various nuclei with sensitive functions related to steroids and glucocorticoids, glucose, and temperature. The hypothalamus also serves as the center of autonomic control. One of its most vital functions, as it is connected to the nervous system and the pituitary gland, a key component of the endocrine homeostasis system, is its neuroendocrine function that affects the autonomic nervous system, thereby maintaining homeostasis of blood pressure, heart rate, body temperature, and consumption behavior, as well as emotions[25].

However, we will not discuss internal homeostasis as it falls within the realm of biology. We will attempt to relate **homeostasis** to **the fight or flight** response. As we know, homeostasis is controlled by the hypothalamus in the brain. The brain receives information from two sources: information from within the body through the nervous system to obtain information about the internal body conditions, and information from outside the body through the senses located throughout the body to obtain information about the external environment.

Conditions outside the body will affect the conditions inside the body. For instance, changes in temperature and climate will automatically alter the body's homeostatic balance, causing the brain to automatically and unconsciously initiate mechanisms to restore the body's homeostasis. For example, when it's hot, the body sweats, and when it's cold, the body shivers.

We will take a step further beyond temperature changes.

The next step is how an imbalance in homeostasis compels an individual to consciously and actively take actions to restore the homeostatic conditions within the body.

This occurs when an individual or organism is in search of food or drink. When an individual feels hungry, there is an imbalance in their homeostasis. The empty stomach sends a signal to the brain that the body needs nourishment, and the brain translates this signal into physical actions of seeking and consuming food.

The same applies when an individual feels thirsty. The body sends a signal to the brain that an imbalance in homeostasis is occurring due to a lack of fluids. The brain receives this signal and translates it into physical activities of seeking water and drinking it to restore the homeostatic balance.

There's a difference in the stages of how an individual restores homeostasis within their body. In the first explanation concerning temperature changes, pH, or humidity, active movement isn't required, and the body automatically carries out activities internally to balance homeostasis, such as automatically sweating when the temperature rises.

In contrast, in the second explanation concerning hunger and thirst, the brain translates this into conscious, active movements by the individual to seek food or drink in order to restore homeostasis within the body. The interesting aspect is that the need for sustenance, for eating and drinking, constitutes a fundamental requirement for life or a drive to live within the id theory. Hence, a conclusion can be drawn that **homeostasis** is indeed related to the basic need to self-preservation in the theory of **the id**.

The drive to live is manifested in the form of maintaining the balance of homeostasis. Alternatively, it can be assumed that in order for an individual to live healthily, the balance of homeostasis must be maintained, which is the task of the hypothalamus. The drive to live is a psychological form of the biological or physiological concept of maintaining homeostatic balance. In other words, the hypothalamus's task of **maintaining homeostasis balance** is the **drive to self-preservation**.

Up to this point, we have assumptions about the relationship between psychology and biology or physiology, which relates to the id theory. The drive for reproduction (development) in psychological concepts is the work of hormones related to sexuality and the functioning of reproductive organs and other active sexual organs. Meanwhile, the drive to self-preservation in psychological concepts is the body's work in maintaining homeostasis within the body. Intriguingly, both the drive for reproduction (development) and the drive to self-preservation are regulated by the hypothalamus, which controls and produces the necessary hormones to create these drives.

Next, we will delve even further by attempting to observe the relationship between the balance of homeostasis and the drive to self-preservation, especially as manifested in the vigilant state, leading to feelings of fear or anger, which prompt the individual to either flee or fight. Before proceeding further, we need to first understand the relationship between the balance of homeostasis, the sympathetic and parasympathetic nerves, and their connection to the senses, before finally linking it to the drive to self-preservation.

In a stable condition, the human body generally maintains balanced homeostasis, where the functions of internal organs work steadily. This stability is maintained by the hypothalamus through the autonomic nervous system, which comprises the sympathetic and parasympathetic nervous systems. The autonomic nervous system is part of the peripheral nervous system, consisting of the somatic nervous system and the autonomic nervous system. Meanwhile, the peripheral nervous system is part of the nervous system, which comprises the central nervous system and the peripheral nervous system[26].

In general, that's how the nervous system in humans

works. However, we won't delve into each component too deeply, but rather, we'll directly examine its functioning based on the topic of discussion.

Simply put, the sympathetic nervous system is responsible for enhancing performance, making individuals more vigilant and energized, while the parasympathetic nervous system is responsible for reducing performance, making individuals more relaxed and at ease. Both systems continuously work to maintain the body's homeostatic balance, enabling it to function effectively and efficiently for as long as possible. This allows the body's organs to cooperate and support each other.

All the functions of the autonomic nervous system go unnoticed by individual consciousness; they work automatically based on the law of homeostatic balance. If there's a change in homeostatic balance, some organ functions will increase, while others will decrease to restore the balance. Once equilibrium is reached, organ functions will return to normal as much as possible[27].

Internal and External Tolerance

Homeostatic balance has a threshold or tolerance for homeostatic equilibrium. In general, the boundaries of homeostatic tolerance can be grouped into two categories: internal tolerance and external tolerance. Internal tolerance boundaries for homeostatic balance are determined by the functioning of the organs within the living organism's body. In the case of humans, these tolerance boundaries are based on the needs of internal organs that collaborate to fulfill their requirements.

A simple example is hunger. When the digestive organs, including the stomach and intestines, require food for digestion, this condition is approaching the threshold of tolerance for these specific digestive organs, as well as the overall homeostatic balance of the body, given the interconnectedness of the body's organs. If this condition is left unattended and food is not provided to the digestive organs, stomach acid levels begin to rise. At this point, the tolerance threshold for homeostatic balance has been reached. If left unchecked, the increased stomach acid can lead to damage, such as ulcers, exceeding the threshold of stomach tolerance and disrupting overall homeostasis, resulting in an imbalance due to stomach injury and causing the individual, in this case a human, to experience discomfort.

When an injury occurs, the hypothalamus instructs the sympathetic and parasympathetic nervous systems to collaborate in increasing and decreasing the performance of organs needed to repair the injury. This helps the body heal and restores homeostatic balance. Insufficient food intake and dehydration are also conditions that can disrupt the balance of internal organ function and overall homeostasis. The entry of viruses, bacteria, or pathogens also disrupts homeostatic balance, especially related to internal organ function.

The achievement of the threshold of tolerance for homeostatic balance is not only based on the endurance and needs of internal organs but also on the body's sensory organs that represent its interaction with the external environment. The level of tolerance or threshold of sensory organs in receiving information or stimuli becomes the threshold of tolerance and homeostatic balance, especially concerning the external environment around the body. The external environment influences the internal environment of the body, and the body's sensory organs act **as extensions** of the internal organs, providing useful information to maintain balanced functioning for the body's internal organs and overall homeostasis.

A common example is the skin's ability to sense temperature in the surrounding environment. The skin acts as the first line of defense in sensing the temperature around the body. When the weather is hot, the information about the hot and uncomfortable temperature is received by the skin's nerves. The heat entering through the skin and other openings affects the homeostatic balance within the body. This leads to an increase in the body's internal temperature, prompting various organs to work together to balance the internal temperature. A common response is sweating.

The body's ability to sense environmental temperature has a threshold. Exceeding this threshold can be dangerous for the individual. Extremely hot or cold environmental temperatures can pose a threat to the individual. When the body feels overheated and begins to surpass the tolerance threshold of the internal organs in maintaining necessary fluids, the individual makes a conscious decision, directed by their thoughts in the brain, to seek water for hydration or move to a place with a more suitable temperature to prevent excessive fluid loss.

The situation of fluid loss due to overheating is a threat to humans as it results in an imbalance of homeostasis. This process demonstrates that the threat of environmental changes, such as an increase in temperature, can disturb homeostatic balance and harm individuals. The aggressive drive for self-preservation or protect oneself from threats is **an effort** to maintain homeostatic balance.

An interesting and different scenario can be observed in the motivation or desire to drink, triggered by two different situations based on the explanation of tolerance thresholds for homeostasis caused by internal and external factors. The first motivation to drink, driven by internal factors, is to maintain homeostatic balance. In this case, the body requires fluid intake to replace fluids used by internal organs for their function and to replace fluids lost through sweat and urine.

On the other hand, the second motivation to drink, driven by external factors, is the threat of hot weather. In this situation, the body requires fluid intake to replace fluids lost due to heat through sweat and evaporation. Drinking serves as a means of survive to prevent dehydration, which can endanger an individual's life.

Next, we will delve further into the self-preservation

drive, exploring the concept of fear or courage as the basis for the fight-or-flight response in the face of threats. Therefore, we will examine these **sensory organs**, which represent the entire body's reception of external information, further, until we discuss memory and perception formed based on the information received by these sensory organs.

Sensory Organs and Reflex Movements

As we know, the self-preservation drive in the form of aggression is preceded by an event or situation outside the individual that affects the individual. However, not all events or situations perceived by the sensory organs trigger the self-preservation drive in the form of aggression. These events or situations must possess specific information that can activate the self-preservation drive in the form of aggression.

As mentioned earlier, a hot temperature within the tolerance threshold of homeostatic balance does not immediately trigger the self-preservation drive in the form of aggression. However, if the temperature becomes excessively hot and leads to dehydration, the self-preservation drive will be activated through actions such as seeking water or moving to a cooler place. Before reaching an excessively high temperature and still within the tolerance threshold of homeostatic balance, an individual may seek water to maintain their homeostasis.

Now, let's consider a scenario that directly presents a threat to the individual. This scenario involves accidentally touching a hot object or getting pierced by a sharp object. This situation causes the hand or foot to immediately retract from the hot or sharp object, resulting in a reflex movement. An interesting point is that reflex movements do not occur in the first example, where the entire body experiences a gradual change in temperature leading to dehydration. However, reflex movements can occur when the entire body, for instance, is subjected to an extreme burn, causing the individual to move uncontrollably in a blind attempt to extinguish the fire on their body, similar to what is often depicted in movies.

The key difference between the first and second examples lies in the speed of information arrival. In the first example, a change in temperature leading to dehydration results in a gradual and corresponding bodily response to restore homeostatic balance. This response starts with the body's attempt to release heat through sweating, followed by the urge to drink, and progresses to dehydration if the situation is not addressed. In extreme cases, this can even lead to death.

In contrast, in the second example, the arrival of information is sudden. The sudden arrival of sensory information immediately damages the tissue affected by the stimulus. Tissue damage **disrupts homeostatic balance**, prompting the body to respond with reflexive movements to withdraw or avoid the source of the stimulus.

These reflex movements are governed by the spinal cord's reflex arc, working automatically. Pain signals from injured or overheated tissues are transmitted to the hypothalamus in the brain, triggering a sensation of pain that stimulates the release of adrenaline hormones[28]. When adrenaline hormone levels increase, the heart rate will rapidly rise, causing a sensation of surprise. The intensity of this surprise depends on the level of pain that affects the action of adrenaline hormone on the heart rate. The more intense the pain, the faster the heart rate, and the more surprised the individual will feel.

The feeling of surprise doesn't occur in the first case because the information received doesn't come suddenly but gradually, according to the surrounding environmental conditions. Additionally, in the case of dehydration due to heat, when it reaches the stage of severe dehydration, the organ's performance is too weakened to respond to adrenaline hormone due to the pain caused by dehydration-induced injuries like abrasions and chapped lips. However, the individual in question could experience shock or a failure of internal organ functions, which could result in death[29].

The event of surprise is a crucial keyword to understand an individual's reaction to threats. Surprise originates from the sudden increase in heart rate due to the action of adrenaline hormone. This hormone also stimulates the brain to think faster and enhances the sensitivity of visual and auditory senses, while the sense of touch becomes numb, which is useful in case of injury to reduce the sensation of pain, allowing energy and concentration to be directed towards staying focused in facing the threat[30].

Let's consider the next example, which involves a threat that also triggers a sense of surprise. The occurrence of lightning or a flash of light accompanied by a loud sound is information that can make an individual feel startled or surprised. The sudden loud sound disrupts the auditory senses, triggering a reflexive movement and stimulating the release of adrenaline hormone, thereby increasing heart rate and causing the individual to feel startled.

Meanwhile, the brain quickly generates thoughts to instruct the hands to cover the ears, reducing the disturbance or discomfort caused by the loud sound. A loud sound received by the auditory senses that approaches or surpasses the threshold of auditory tolerance induces a reflexive action in the individual, such as opening the mouth to alleviate pressure on the auditory senses. This reflexive action is controlled by the spinal cord[31].

The condition of loud noise constitutes a threat that can disrupt homeostatic balance, particularly concerning the sense of hearing. An individual's response to exposure to loud noise is to protect their auditory senses through reflexive movements and rapid reactions from the brain. If we look at it from the fight or flight perspective, the process of self-protection can be regarded as a reflexive movement to **flight** for safety.

The process that unfolds is self-preservation first, to prevent or minimize damage from the threatening stimulus. The self-preservation response is a reaction from reflexive movements that work automatically and quick brain responses. Subsequently, the adrenal glands release adrenaline hormones depending on the level of damage and the intensity of pain.

Reflexive movements, regulated by the spinal cord, are the fundamental response to stimuli that harm the sensory organs in the human body. However, reflexive movements don't only function in response to injury; they have a basic role as an extension of automatic movements regulated by the spinal cord, collaborating with the hypothalamus to maintain the body's homeostatic balance.

The spinal cord and hypothalamus possess absolute control that cannot be consciously regulated in managing various internal organs in the body, which function to maintain homeostatic balance. These reflexive movements serve as an extension of the spinal cord's reach, interacting with external conditions or factors outside the body that might disturb bodily homeostasis. This applies to stimuli that have already damaged body tissues, like wounds, as well as other reflex functions aimed at preserving body form or posture. For instance, when the body is pushed, the muscles will reflexively contract to maintain body position and balance[32].

However, when the stimulus causes pain or damage to the body, it's not just reflexive movements that come into play; the adrenaline system also reacts, where the stimulus is reported to the hypothalamus in the brain, which then activates the adrenaline system.

Reflexive movements are not limited to avoiding or "fleeing," they can also take the form of aggressive reflexes or "fight" responses. Aggressive reflexes emerge when pleasure is threatened. Threats to pleasure cause individuals to feel obstructed in enjoying their pleasures, leading them to respond aggressively to maintain and continue their pleasure.

The distinction between avoidance reflexes and aggressive reflexes mainly lies in sensory stimuli. If avoidance reflexes are stimulated by sensory damage, such as the skin being exposed to heat, aggressive reflexes are triggered by the sudden cessation of sensory stimulation.

For instance, when engrossed in eating, the sense of taste is being stimulated. Suddenly, the pleasure-inducing stimulus is interrupted as someone takes away the food. The body's automatic reaction is an aggressive reflex, aimed at reclaiming the food. This principle applies to other sensory stimuli like sex or engaging in enjoyable activities.

Actually the body automatically halts sensory stimulation once satisfaction is achieved. For example, after being satiated, food no longer tastes good, or after reaching the peak of pleasure during sexual activity, the body is no longer responsive to sexual stimuli. The same applies to playing games; if one becomes fatigued, the desire to play diminishes. However, if satisfaction hasn't been reached and stimulation is halted prematurely, aggressive reflexes come into play to ensure that sensory stimulation is satisfactorily fulfilled.

So from this, there are two distinctions in reflexive movements. The first is the avoidance reflex, aimed at survival, which represents a threat to the instinct for self-preservation. The second is the aggressive reflex, aimed at pleasure retention, which represents a threat to the instinct for development.

Hence, aggressive behavior for self-preservation is more accurately an avoidance reflex, referred to as the **survival** drive, which focuses on sustaining life. Meanwhile, the aggressive reflex to **pleasure retention** falls within the instinct for development. Thus, the current categorization of the id :

- **Drive for development**
  - **Fight for pleasure retention**
- **Drive for self-preservation**
  - **Flight for survival**

Reflexive movements can be conditioned through a process that begins with conscious movements but can transform into reflexive actions through appropriate training[33]. The learned reflexive movements are part of the central nervous system, which is more complex in terms of the collaboration between the brain and the spinal cord, compared to simple reflex movements controlled solely by the spinal cord.

The adrenaline system also doesn't only function in cases of injury or damage, but it's stimulated by loud sounds, pain, light, speed, height due to gravitational pull, and most importantly, perception[34]. The primary function of this adrenaline system is to prepare the body to face stimuli in the form of threats, both existing and potential ones, and not just to prepare responses for fight or flight.

The adrenaline system activated by the hypothalamus is only aimed at preparing the body, that is, to be vigilant or increase awareness, and then respond with flight or fight. The adrenaline system serves as the button for being **vigilant** or increasing awareness, and once again, it is not a response for flight or fight. This understanding is very important and is one of the key mysteries that will be revealed.

Awareness and Vigilance

The spinal cord and the hypothalamus have a **monitoring function** to maintain the body's homeostasis balance to function for as long as possible or to stay alive for as long as possible. This monitoring function is the working principle of the drive to self-preservation, called the **principle of awareness**. The principle of awareness is the second principle in the id, in addition to the principle of pleasure.

The operation of this awareness principle runs automatically based on stimulus and response, namely maintaining the working condition of organs in carrying out homeostasis functions to remain within the limits of homeostasis balance tolerance.

The condition of organs within the body in carrying out homeostasis functions is influenced by three factors: based on the activities of the body's internal organs themselves, based on stimuli that enter the body such as food, air, or particles or microorganisms such as bacteria or viruses, and then based on external stimuli in the form of information received by the body's senses.

However, if external stimulus information begins to disrupt internal homeostasis balance, such as information that exceeds the threshold of the senses like having a skin injury, sound that is too loud, or being at a height that disrupts body balance, then the hypothalamus will work to activate a state of vigilance in the body, thus increasing vigilance from an automatic stimulus and response state to individual consciousness, manifesting as being **vigilant** about the external environment.

In the next stage, when the monitoring function is in the conscious or controlled state, the individual has the ability to assess the situation they are facing, whether they perceive the threat as having passed or not. If it has passed, then the individual will return to a state of calm, but if they still perceive a danger that threatens them, they will make decisions to protect themselves based on their perception, whether they choose to flee, fight, or just defend themselves.

An example of a situation where vigilance is required, but the threat quickly subsides, is when we are walking and suddenly hear a motorcycle horn. Our body suddenly becomes alert, but afterward, the body reduces the level of alertness it is experiencing by returning the heart rate and other related bodily systems to normal.

However, if the motorcycle that honked the horn comes closer to us, our body will react to avoid the approaching motorcycle, which is a survival reaction. Afterward, the individual can either remain calm or even become angry, taking off their sandals or shoes to throw them in the direction of the motorcyclist while expressing frustration. This reaction can be categorized as a confrontational stance.

Returning to the basic function of survival and pleasure retention, forms of flight or fight are subsequent responses and are not initial instincts or drives. Meanwhile, the initial response in the form of flight or fight is a state of **vigilance**.

This state of vigilance can be accompanied by reflex movements involving avoiding or protecting oneself if the threat has occurred and has disrupted or endangered the body's senses, And the aggressive reflex kicks in when there is a threat to pleasure or enjoyment. However, it can also occur without reflex movements if the threat in question is a **perception** formed within the mind. For example, upon hearing a dangerous story such as a robbery, the body automatically becomes vigilant due to the perception of robbery, which is a form of threat.

The adrenaline system activated by the hypothalamus serves as the button to make the body vigilant or alert. This state of vigilance is crucial and serves as a fundamental principle for living beings, especially for survival and pleasure retention. **This principle of vigilance** is the third principle in the id, alongside **the pleasure principle** in the drive for development and **the principle of awareness** in the drive to self-preservation. Thus, within humans, there are **three principles** that motivate.

As explained earlier, the principle of vigilance is a system that operates before making decisions for flight or fight in the face of threats. Before deciding to flight or fight, or take other actions, the decision-making is also influenced by perception in the individual's mind regarding the existing threat. Therefore, let's now explore how perception leads to the necessary decisions in facing threats.

CHAPTER 5
PERCEPTION

It's better for us to first understand the definition of perception that I've quoted from Wikipedia. Perception (from the Latin word "perceptio", "percipio") is the act of organizing, recognizing, and interpreting sensory information to provide a picture and understanding of the environment. Perception includes all signals in the nervous system, which are the result of physical or chemical stimulation of sensory organs. For example, vision involves light hitting the retina in the eye, smell utilizes odor molecules (aromas), and hearing involves sound waves.

Perception is not a passive reception of signals, but it is shaped by learning, memory, expectations, and attention[35]. Perception arising from information received by individuals will determine actions or responses based on that stimulus, including responses to threat stimuli. After previously using the sense of hearing as an example, we will now use the sense of sight to understand how the perception of threat is formed and develops into the decision to fight or flee, as well as its connection to the principle of vigilance.

Humans become vigilant when they see certain animals, such as dogs, large cats, or even smaller creatures like cockroaches and spiders. If encountering large animals like dogs or big cats, it is reasonable for humans to be cautious, assuming that these animals could pose a threat.

But what about insects or other creatures much smaller

than humans? Why do humans also become vigilant towards them? Is the answer the same, that these creatures could harm humans? Let's return to the primary function of the sense of sight, which is to receive visual information.

Visual information received by the sense of sight provides information to the brain. Some of this information is processed into perceptions, and if these perceptions are interpreted as threats, the individual becomes vigilant. However, some information doesn't require conscious perception; the individual becomes vigilant automatically.

In the case of the sense of hearing, loud noises trigger this response; similarly, for the sense of sight, height or looking down triggers this response. Vigilance towards height is related to visual information that is automatically interpreted by the spinal cord, which triggers reflexive movements to maintain body balance.

The reflexive movement that maintains body balance in response to height works automatically and can be learned. This is different from walking on a flat surface, where the level of vigilance is lower. Conversely, the steeper the descent or slope, the more vigilant we become, increasing the release of adrenaline. Vigilance is necessary to maintain balance and prevent falling.

The explanation above only covers vigilance when descending from a height, but it turns out that animals or humans, even without descending, are vigilant just by looking from a height. This is due to the presence of visual proprioception in the brain, which provides information to the spinal cord to prepare reflexive movements that help maintain body position and balance when the body is in motion.

Visual proprioception is the formation of visual stimulus perception related to the recognition of the body's position in relation to the surrounding situation, including the activation of muscles related to body balance[36]. The spinal cord, in preparing reflex movements, operates automatically based on data originating from the brain and functions in the subconscious mind. Even if we don't plan to descend from a height, the body has already readied the necessary reflex muscle movements, and the higher the distance of the descent, the greater the vigilance.

An example of this is when we are atop a tree, especially as children. When we look around, we enjoy the beautiful scenery. However, when we look down, the body becomes vigilant even if there's no intention to descend, and when we do descend, it's done cautiously with a high level of vigilance.

Because this height vigilance operates in the subconscious, we don't need to consciously be vigilant; the body is automatically vigilant. This is a form of innate vigilance brought since birth, thanks to visual proprioception in the brain, which works automatically.

Essentially, it's visual proprioception in the brain that provides height information to the spinal cord. While this situation is formed through the sense of sight, if the sense of sight is disrupted, the body relies on other senses, like touch, to create proprioception based on touch. Proprioception is how the body knows where it is in any given situation[37] through information from various senses, both consciously and unconsciously.

The sense of vision, apart from being the gateway for information that makes individuals cautious about heights, is also sensitive to rapid movements that cannot be tracked by the eyes. Fast and sudden movements are one of the reasons why humans are cautious about insects like cockroaches, for instance. Information received suddenly or seeing movements that are too swift through the sense of vision causes the brain to lack accurate and sufficient information about the seen object, particularly its presumed position.

This uncertainty in information prompts the sense of vision to increase its sensitivity, thus making the body more vigilant. Humans will never be able to keep up with changes in the cockroach's movement direction because the cockroach's reaction speed is much faster than the blink of a human eye[38].

As a result, we are always startled when the cockroach changes its direction of movement, or at the very least, the sensitivity of the human visual senses increases, leading the individual to become more alert.

Besides cockroaches, being in a fast-moving car also increases the sensitivity of the sense of vision. This is because the brain does not receive precise information about one's own position relative to the surrounding environment, which is crucial for preparing reflexive balance movements, as explained earlier, as well as determining the position of objects being observed.

Through the sense of vision, humans can enjoy the beauty of nature, but on the other hand, they may feel uncomfortable or dislike being in a cluttered or dirty environment. Humans will not be vigilant when they perceive beauty, even if it involves new information. For example, let's compare a scenario where a person is in the mountains with breathtakingly beautiful views, to a scenario where a person is in a messy or dirty environment, or in a creepy forest with dense, damp trees. The result is that individuals in a beautiful environment will not be vigilant, while those in a cluttered or dirty environment will be more vigilant.

We can also observe that humans tend to be more vigilant when they see someone with a disheveled appearance and an unattractive or fierce face. Conversely, they may be less vigilant when encountering someone with a beautiful or handsome face, even though both individuals, whether unattractive or attractive, are strangers. This aspect is often exploited by marketing strategies.

In essence, humans prefer harmony, tidiness, and beauty, while they dislike disorder, dirtiness, and untidiness. Balance, beauty, harmony, and peace create conditions that enhance human self-preservation opportunities compared to environments filled with conflicts, disharmony, frequent quarrels, or wars. **The balance in the external environment** contributes to **the balance within the body**, and vice versa.

Imposing stimuli, such as loud noises, dazzling lights, sudden movements, looking downward from a height, being in a high-speed car, viewing something dirty, filthy, or cluttered, and many others, lead to heightened sensory awareness, making individuals more alert.

These pieces of information, besides enhancing sensory awareness, also interconnect and form perceptions that are processed by the brain. Perception involves advanced cognitive processes that are not only active when responding but are also shaped through learning. Perception is a fundamental imaginative process that combines different pieces of information from experiences and learning.

A common example of combined learning from two different sensory inputs affecting two different senses is the flash of lightning and the sound of thunder. In this scenario, people are alert when they see lightning, preparing to hear the loud sound of thunder, because they have learned from previous experiences that lightning is followed by thunder.

Human intelligence develops over time, and the development of perception becomes increasingly complex, influenced by factors such as intelligence, experience, education, culture, upbringing, and other factors that can shape perception.

This time, we're presenting two complex and contrasting perceptions. The first perception pertains to human attraction to individuals with attractive or handsome appearances, driven by the principle of pleasure, influenced by sexual instincts. The second perception is formed through a learning process, involving human vigilance toward unfamiliar individuals, driven by the survival instincts.

These two perceptions converge when a person is approached by a stranger with a charming appearance. In this situation, there is a conflict between the pleasure principle and the vigilance principle. If the pleasure principle dominates, the individual will be captivated by the attractiveness of the stranger, feeling fascinated or entranced. However, if the vigilance principle prevails, the individual will be cautious or vigilant, trying not to be influenced by the stranger's attractiveness and instead adopting a neutral or cautious stance while awaiting further information about the person. There is one more possibility: the individual may become fearful of the stranger or react defensively, harboring negative assumptions and suspicions about the attractive stranger.

In the final possibility, the perception of an object in a specific situation can be perceived as a threat, but it can also be perceived differently, such as an opportunity or chance. Perception is formed based on external stimuli and responds based on the inherent drives in the id, whether it's the drive for development with the principle of pleasure, or the drive for flight or fight with the principle of vigilance. Next, we will delve into each of these perceptions that influence the drives within the id. We will start by discussing the perception of threats first, as the transformation of the death instinct into the flight or fight instinct is our main focus, followed by a discussion of perceptions based on the pleasure principle.

CHAPTER 6
PERCEPTION AND VIGILANCE

As humans age, their perceptions of the environment around them become increasingly complex. An individual's perception of a situation, object, event, or incident can vary based on their experiences and learning. It can be perceived as a threat or in various other ways. For instance, consider the perception of a person towards a dog being taken for a walk by its owner.

The first person perceives the dog as friendly, approaches it, and shows affection. Meanwhile, the second person perceives the dog as aggressive and tries to stay away. If the dog is indeed friendly, the first person experiences the pleasure of interacting with a friendly dog, while the second person misses out on the opportunity to enjoy the company of a friendly dog. However, if the dog turns out to be aggressive, the first person suffers the consequence of being bitten, while the second person avoids the dog's bite.

When the first person gets bitten by the dog, they learn that a chained and walked dog can pose a threat. As a result, a perception of threat towards that dog is formed. If the person encounters a dog again, they will be cautious. However, if the person becomes traumatized by the dog's bite, they might react in fear upon seeing a dog.

Based on gains and risks, simple logic suggests that more people would avoid the dog rather than approach it. The risk of getting bitten by the dog outweighs the chance to interact with it. Perception of threat is shaped by experiences and learning, including upbringing, education, culture, and even religion.

Perceiving a threat causes individuals to become vigilant, and this vigilance can transform into fear through processes that influence the brain's functioning. The transformation from vigilance to fear is one of the mysteries that sheds light on the nature of emotions. One important hypothesis is that the emotion of fear is not one of the basic human emotions but rather an advanced form of vigilance. To put it more extremely, the emotion of fear can be seen as a **disturbance** of the survival-based vigilance principle.

Next, we will explore how this vigilance principle transforms into the emotion of fear, and not just fear but also includes anger. The explanation I will provide is currently speculative and not yet supported by scientific research, as there are many experts who believe that humans have a number of basic emotions. Some suggest there are four basic emotions, while others propose six basic emotions[39] and there are also those who say that humans have inherent fear emotions, namely fear of heights and fear of loud noises[40].

However, as explained in the previous chapters, I prefer the use of the term "vigilance" in relation to heights and loud noises rather than the emotion of fear. Let's embark on the next adventure.

Threats and Vigilance

Memory and experience are closely related to the formation of perceptions that can make humans vigilant or even fearful. There are two parts of the brain that play a role in storing memories: the amygdala and the hippocampus. The amygdala is a cluster of almond-shaped nerve cells. The amygdala is believed to be the part of the brain that processes and stores emotional reactions[41].

The hippocampus is a part of the large brain located in the temporal lobe. The hippocampus plays a role in memory and spatial navigation. The term "hippocampus" is derived from its shape in coronal sections, which resembles a seahorse. In Alzheimer's disease, the hippocampus is the brain region that is first affected; difficulties in memory and loss of orientation are its main symptoms[42]. The process of transforming vigilance into fear is closely related to memory, especially the amygdala. The following is the process of this transformation.

One day, a human faces an event, situation, or object that is perceived as a threat for the first time. When this information reaches the threshold of homeostatic balance tolerance, the hypothalamus in the brain activates a response of vigilance related to that threat. This response involves the activation of the adrenal glands to release necessary hormones, namely adrenaline and cortisol.

Adrenaline and noradrenaline hormones make the individual more vigilant, increasing the reception of information through the senses[43], his thinking ability also increases due to the additional energy from glucose in the blood that rises in the brain, a result of the action of cortisol hormone breaking down sugar reserves in the liver to provide energy for the brain, enhancing cognitive performance. This heightened energy also reaches the muscles, boosting muscle strength to enable maximum reactions when facing a threat[44].

When the brain is stimulated with a vigilant response, a substantial amount of energy originating from glucose in the blood causes the cells within the brain to work harder, leading to faster thinking. In this situation, these cells can become fatigued and are at risk of malfunction, potentially triggering self-destruct commands from the overworked brain cells. This prompts the replacement of these exhausted cells with fresher ones, especially within the hippocampal cell tissue associated with memory[45].

Furthermore, cortisol hormone, along with adrenaline

hormone in the brain, will form **memories** associated with **emotional events**[46] in the form of bodily responses related to the body's homeostasis balancing process against the stimuli received by the senses, both perceived as threats and stimuli. These memories are stored in the amygdala, while the experiences and learning of how to respond to these stimuli are stored in the hippocampus[47]. This memory is useful for dealing with threat or stimulus situations. Next, we will delve into the following explanation, where we will focus more on the perception of threats to uncover the secrets of the principle of vigilance.

When a human has previously experienced a threatening situation and has a memory of that threat, then when a similar threat arises again, the brain will not react as it did during the first encounter with the threat. The threat information received by the brain through the body's senses will reach the hippocampus, where the amygdala is located.

Then, in the amygdala, a process of retrieving memories related to the body's response to threats occurs, also known as **emotional memory**. This pertains to events that have the potential to disrupt the body's homeostasis balance and is based on past memories to confront the current threat being faced[48].

The body's response activated by the amygdala constitutes information of homeostatic imbalance for the hypothalamus based on the perception of threat processed by the amygdala. As a result, the hypothalamus activates the adrenaline system in response to this perceived threat, leading to an increase in the principle of vigilance. Once it reaches the hypothalamus, the process is similar to when an individual encounters a threat for the first time.

The difference between the first encounter with a threat and a subsequent one lies in the fact that in the first threat, the incoming sensory information immediately causes a homeostatic imbalance that prompts the hypothalamus to activate the adrenaline system. In contrast, in the second threat, the sensory information is first processed by the amygdala, perceiving it as a threat that disrupts homeostasis, thereby leading the hypothalamus to activate the adrenaline system **based on perception**. This is different from the first threat, where the hypothalamus activates the adrenaline system based on information that has crossed the threshold of homeostatic balance tolerance, such as threats like loud noises or pain from an injury.

After the adrenaline system is activated and the body responds to the threat, both in the first and second threats, the body's response, actions taken against the threat, and the threat itself are stored in both the amygdala and the hippocampus **as memories**. In the case of the second threat, the brain **doesn't need to think again** like it did during the first encounter with a threat because the thought patterns that lead to the actions have already been recorded in memory. The brain only needs to think about **improving and strengthening** the necessary actions to make the response more efficient and effective. Thoughts that lead to actions as a response to a threat will be recorded in the amygdala, and if repeated, they can become an automatic form of response called a reflex motion, which is **learned** in the face of threats.

One example of a reflex motion learned in the face of threats is in boxing. A boxer trains reflex motions when facing the threat of an opponent's attack. When the threat comes in the form of a punch from the opponent, the boxer trains to evade or block as a reflex motion, which can then be followed by a counter punch. If this evasive motion followed by a counter punch is trained extensively, it can become an automatic motion or reflex for the boxer when facing a threat like a punch from the opponent. There are many other examples of learned reflex motions, such as driving a car, riding a bicycle, and especially in military training processes.

Fear

Repetitive threats can be learned to generate actions that

are more effective and efficient in facing threats. However, continuous threats or pressures can cause individuals to become stressed and overwhelmed, and they can transform the principle of vigilance towards a threat into fear. It is from pressures or threats like these that fear, the **greatest enemy** of mankind, emerges.

The process of changing vigilance into fear begins with the arrival of threats. As explained above, when a threat is present, cortisol hormone functions to activate a self-destructive response in brain cells that have become fatigued, which will be replaced by new, fresher cells. In the case of consecutive threats, cortisol hormone continues to circulate in the brain, carrying out its function when the next threat arrives. This condition results in an accumulation of cortisol, inhibiting the critical and rapid thinking functions of the brain that are stimulated by adrenaline. This is because the brain cells, especially in the hippocampus region, are still tired and are undergoing the self-destructive process induced by residual cortisol from the previous threat production[49]. As a result, the individual fails to access the memories in the hippocampus to retrieve the knowledge and experiences needed to deal with the threat they are facing[50].

As a consequence, the individual relies primarily on the body's response memory from the amygdala originating from previous threats, coupled with a limited capacity of logical thinking. However, memories related to past events, thoughts, and actions when facing the threat can only be accessed to a small extent. The result is certainly not as effective and efficient as when the brain can function at its fullest and memories from previous threats can be accessed maximally.

Even though the incoming threat is similar to the previous one, there are always distinct details that provide different experiences for the individual because no threat is exactly the same. The consequence of this is that the individual finds it **harder to think clearly** in pressured situations. Consequently, the memories stored in the amygdala and hippocampus subsequently have **lower quality** in terms of responsive reactions to threats compared to previous memories.

Then, in a relatively short time, the next threat arrives, where the amount of cortisol continues to accumulate in the brain while brain cells are still fatigued and those that are no longer functioning normally are being signaled to self-destruct by the cortisol hormone. This situation leads to a decreasing number of cells ready for clear thinking, and the access to hippocampus for retrieving learning memories from past experiences cannot be accessed, resulting in thinking failure. As a result, the brain solely relies on the body's response memory from the amygdala, which **lacks effectiveness** in facing threats due to inadequately resolved previous threat incidents. This leads to actions that do not provide solutions, and the emerging thoughts are **blank**, where the brain is **incapable of thinking at all** and the body's response memory does **not effectively** respond to the necessary actions in facing the threat.

Usually, the response that occurs when the body's response memory is still sufficiently functional involves fleeing clumsily, potentially accompanied by urination or even defecation in order to evade the threat[51]. When the body's response memory becomes increasingly ineffective, the subconscious mind will attempt to delve into the past where the individual could find a sense of security and assistance in facing threats during childhood or infancy, namely by crying[52].

Some individuals even faint, a condition caused by the nervous system in the brain experiencing disruption. However, the nervous system's role is to regulate various functions of organs throughout the body. Due to this nervous system disturbance, the heartbeat slows down and blood vessels in the legs dilate. As a result, blood flows downward to the legs, causing a sudden drop in blood pressure. Consequently, the brain doesn't receive sufficient blood and oxygen supply. This is what leads to the individual fainting[53].

Then, the memory of the threat along with actions that didn't provide a solution is stored again in the amygdala in the form of the body's response memory, which we call **the emotion of fear**. Of course, the hippocampus will record this experience of fear. In this state, the individual already possesses a **memory of failure** in dealing with threats along with its consequences and the losses resulting from that failure, which we refer to as **fear**.

At this point, the **principle of vigilance changes into fear**. The transition from vigilance to fear doesn't even need to reach the point of fainting. Difficult situations in thinking or going **blank** can already trigger panic and transform the principle of vigilance into the emotion of fear.

If, later on, the individual who already has a memory of the emotion of fear faces a threat, then it's the memory of the emotion of fear that emerges with all of its behaviors, even if the individual is not in a high-pressure situation where cortisol hormone is urging the cells in the hippocampus to commit suicide. However, the memory of the emotion of fear, combined with the recollection of fearful experiences in the hippocampus, which contains an inability to think, instructs the brain not to think either, resulting in a fear response in the individual and rendering them incapable of dealing with the threat. This condition is what's referred to as an **amygdala hijack**[54].

This condition can occur because when the memory of the emotion of fear emerges, there is no solution to address the threat. Within the memory of the emotion of fear, there is no thinking that results in action; instead, it contains an inability to think. As a result, the threat continues to exist, and the amygdala accesses this memory of fear again, instructing the brain not to think based on the command from the hippocampal memory that contains an inability to think. Consequently, fear grows and accumulates.

This is different from the memory of the body's vigilant response, where it provides solutions to threats through necessary actions for quick or immediate responses. Afterward, there's no need to access the memory again since a solution already exists. Instead, the subsequent access involves logical thinking skills to enhance the efficiency or effectiveness of the vigilant response previously executed by the body, along with the necessary actions to address the threat.

In short, the difference between the memory of the emotion of fear and vigilance is that when in fear, **the brain loses its ability to think**, while in vigilance, **the brain's performance actually improves**. However, there's a slight difference in babies, particularly in terms of brain performance, as a baby's thinking capacity is vastly different from that of adults.

Vigilance and Fear in Babies

Babies have a simple thought pattern that relies on crying as a response to threats or dangers. In threatened situations, such as feeling hungry or overheated, a baby will cry to get attention from adults or parents to address the issue. When a baby feels threatened, adrenaline increases, causing the baby to cry loudly. If the parents promptly help the baby address the problem, the behavior of crying and the subsequent assistance from parents are recorded in the amygdala and hippocampus as a solution for the baby to face the threat. This stored memory is a form of **vigilance** in babies when confronting threats or discomfort.

However, when parents are unable to help the baby overcome the issue, and the baby continues to cry loudly without finding a resolution, what gets stored is the behavior of crying loudly that didn't lead to a solution. This **memory without a solution** transforms the baby's vigilance into fear, specifically, the memory of emotional reactions that's recorded in the amygdala but without a solution. Eventually, this marks the first time a human child experiences fear. This fear will diminish the belief that parents can provide assistance or a sense of security, and if parents continually fail to provide the needed help, this fear will evolve into various advanced psychological disturbances.

Advanced-Level Fear

Fear can become the beginning of a greater fear towards the same threat and can evolve into a broader and diverse fear of other forms of threats, which may further develop into other psychological disorders. This sequence of events can unfold as follows:

When the initial fear emerges, the brain becomes incapable of efficient and effective thinking in facing the threat. This incapability is recorded in the memory of the body's fear response in the amygdala, and the experience of the fearful event along with the learning from it is stored in the hippocampus. Similarly, when the next threat arises, the memory of the fear emotion and its experience resurfaces, and the brain once again fails to think logically to overcome the threat. This situation is then recorded in memory to prepare for the next encounter with a threat, and this cycle continues.

The continual reinforcement of the fear memory, coupled with the inability to think logically to counter the threat, causes the individual to lose their ability to confront threats. This leads to an escalation of fear towards threats.

As other threats emerge, even if they are different from the original source of fear, the individual's pre-existing significant fear contributes to a diminished ability to think clearly, and they might experience varying degrees of fear, even if the threats differ.

With repeated exposure to new threats and the presence of the fear emotion memory, new fear memories can develop for different types of threats. This process can lead the individual to become fearful of various threats, a state often referred to as being **overly fearful** or "chicken shit." Certain situations can lead to an extremely high level of fear towards one specific threat, often referred to as trauma.

Fear can develop into anxiety, causing the individual to start feeling disturbed and having difficulty leading a healthy everyday life. This anxiety can evolve into various other psychological disorders. Fear, of course, can be alleviated through therapy or counseling with experts in the field. A simple way to address fear is by **rationalizing** the situation within the threat when the individual is no longer in a threatened or fearful state.

After analyzing the actions that should be taken when facing a threat, the individual can attempt to confront the fear-inducing threat again. The individual will likely feel fear once more, and then the analysis can be repeated after not feeling fearful, followed by facing the threat again repeatedly in this manner. Eventually, the individual will cease to experience fear and instead become **vigilant** when facing the threat. This will replace the body's fear response with a **vigilant response**, and this process can be reinforced over time, enabling the individual to overcome fear and think clearly when confronting threats. Of course, during threat exposure exercises, a significant time gap should be maintained, and threats or pressures should not come in rapid succession, ensuring that there is no accumulation of cortisol in the individual's brain.

Anger

The principle of vigilance that results in vigilant memory not only can turn into fear but also into anger. This condition is related to the fight response. There are two conditions explaining why the fight response occurs.

1. Perception Change

This condition occurs when the body's response memory within the amygdala shifts from vigilance to fear, and subsequently, when facing a subsequent threat, it can shift from the emotion of fear to the emotion of anger because the source of the threat is perceived as **inferior** to the individual.

When the brain is unable to think clearly due to fear, yet the threat source is deemed inferior to the individual, the individual might develop a sense of superiority. The feeling of being pressured or threatened within them transforms into an uncontrollable aggressive attitude due to the diminished role of logic or the brain's ability to think clearly. However, not all instances of fear can transform into anger. Apart from the threat source being inferior, the individual in question must not be excessively dominated by fear, or they must still possess some degree of thinking capacity, at least enough to make a decision to act aggressively in the face of the threat.

However, if the individual is entirely overwhelmed by fear, they won't be able to act aggressively to turn fear into anger. Additionally, individuals who have undergone severe trauma from a single event won't be able to act aggressively to transform fear into anger. Once an individual becomes acquainted with and experiences anger, this emotion will be stored in the amygdala as a memory of the emotional or bodily response to **anger**.

When a threat arises, and the threat source is perceived as inferior to the individual, what immediately emerges is not fear or fear that later turns into anger, but rather the memory of the emotion of anger surfaces directly to address the threat.

The distinction between fear and anger lies in the fact that extreme fear won't offer a solution to incoming threats, and it only subsides after the threat dissipates, or it might offer a solution if the individual is still able to think to some extent and isn't completely dominated by extreme fear. In such cases, the individual might flee clumsily or seek shelter to avoid the threat. Conversely, anger provides a solution in the form of aggressive actions to confront the threat, and the higher the level of anger they possess, the more aggressive the actions taken to address the threat. Anger consistently provides a solution, which contrasts with fear where higher levels of fear offer less solution, and the ultimate outcome might be unconsciousness.

Based on its emergence, it can be said that anger arising from a perception change from fear is an aggressive action that emerges from a **change in the perception of fear** into an aggressive form that lacks or reduces the ability to think clearly or logically. Individuals dominated by fear and anger will experience fear when facing a superior threat and will feel anger when the threat is perceived as inferior to them. Naturally, the perception of threat, feelings of superiority, or inferiority are subjective to each individual.

For instance, consider a child deeply engrossed in playing with a mobile phone who is then reprimanded by their parent. However, the child responds by getting angry at the parent, viewing the parent's position as inferior to their own. As a result, the child becomes more aggressive towards the parent. This situation might arise from the parent excessively spoiling the child or frequently allowing the child to act aggressively without offering guidance or encouraging logical thinking, which is a characteristic of vigilant behavior. Consequently, the child's aggressive behavior ends up being directed towards the parent because the child perceives themselves as superior to the parent.

2. Threat of Pleasure Principle

Anger can also be related to the principle of pleasure, in the form of threats that obstruct or delay the attainment of desired enjoyment. Thus, threats are no longer perceived merely as forms of harm or injury, but can also be perceived as obstacles preventing the attainment of something, risking the failure to obtain or achieve it.

For instance, anger in the form of frustration arises when there is a desire to acquire something one wants, but it is unsuccessful or encounters specific obstacles, leading to a lack of satisfaction. This can manifest as a feeling of being thwarted in pursuing one's desires, resulting in a sense of anger. When we desire something to gain pleasure or enjoyment, dopamine[55] will generate motivation in the form of energy to strive for that pleasure. However, if the desire is not fulfilled, this energy accumulates and can lead to increased aggressiveness in pursuing that desire.

Of course, this aggressive behavior can arise because obstacles or hindrances are perceived as threats to pleasure, thus carrying the potential for the failure to attain that pleasure. In this context, adrenaline triggers such aggressive actions. Therefore, within the person pursuing pleasure, both dopamine and adrenaline are present simultaneously, typically resulting in a feeling of excitement. For instance, when approaching a desired romantic partner, the initial excitement might turn into frustration if progress is hindered, leading to a sense of unease. Or it might even turn into annoyance, as the outcome doesn't align with expectations, resulting in a strategic retreat. This aggressive behavior can be displayed through vigilance or anger, or even a combination of both, where anger and vigilance coexist.

The process of shifting from vigilance to anger is analogous to the transformation from vigilance to fear. In both cases, prolonged exposure to threats diminishes the capacity for clear thinking. The second shift to anger can be due to an inability to think and find solutions to cope with the threat. This could be due to a lack of cognitive development, as seen in children or infants, or it might result from excessively complex threats that are difficult to strategize against.

.....

The transformation of vigilance into fear and anger due to threats to personal safety or pleasure creates a diverse and intriguing spectrum of human behavior. The same stimulus can evoke varying responses, such as vigilance, fear, or anger.

For example, in school-aged children, while taking an exam, some might feel fearful of failing to complete it, while others might become frustrated for not being able to answer the questions. Their reactions will differ accordingly; a fearful child might cry, whereas a frustrated child might become angry or even have a tantrum.

For both the fearful and the frustrated child, it's possible to maintain a vigilant stance without falling into the depths of fear or frustration. They can remain vigilant without succumbing to fear even when faced with punishment or maintain vigilance without succumbing to frustration despite the risk of failing to receive a reward.

The question then becomes, which approach is more effective for taking exams? Neither approach is particularly effective when the primary motivation is avoiding punishment or obtaining a reward. While rewards and punishments can serve as supplementary motivators, they should not be the main driving force. The primary motivation for taking exams should be the pursuit of learning itself, driven by the curiosity to acquire knowledge, not studying merely for rewards or to evade punishment.

Numerous other examples exist regarding the development of fear and anger. However, the main focus isn't on these examples, but rather on the explanation above, which positions fear and anger as **disturbances** of the vigilance principle within the id. This viewpoint contradicts the widely held belief in society that fear and anger are natural and normal emotions. Some studies even classify fear and anger as basic human emotions.

This perspective opens up new possibilities or alternatives for viewing the emotions of fear and anger from a different angle. Fear is a disturbance of the vigilance principle, as individuals experience continuous psychological pressure. Consequently, there is a chance or possibility to avoid experiencing the disturbance of fear altogether or even to eliminate the concept of fear entirely in the future. This could lead to a civilization free from fear, categorizing fear as a treatable and avoidable mental condition, much like headaches or other physical ailments.

CHAPTER 7 FEAR

Since ancient times, our civilization has coexisted with fear and integrated it into our daily lives. We often hear various expressions about fear such as "don't be afraid," "fear is natural," "fear is humanity's main enemy," "overcome fear," and other similar sayings. Fear has, to some extent, influenced the development of human civilization, impacting various aspects of life including economics, religion, education, governance, sports, and nearly every facet of existence.

Fear plays a role in decision-making; it is also used by rulers to control their subjects and leaders to manage their subordinates. Fear is employed as a tool of mass control, used to influence the public or society as a whole.

Almost all humans on Earth are accustomed to fear and accept it as a normal emotion in daily life. We are used to hearing the statement that it is natural for humans to feel fear. However, based on the explanation in the previous chapter, it is shown that fear is **learned** and is a **disturbance** of the principle of vigilance. This implies that humans can actually be **free from fear** if they are nurtured and educated correctly.

In the future, human civilization could potentially be freed from fear. Fear or apprehension will be treated as a mental disturbance similar to anxiety, paranoia, greed, and various other mental disorders that could lead to more severe psychological conditions like depression or schizophrenia, just as with anger. Every individual will become aware of the dangers of fear and anger and take precautions to avoid succumbing to them, much like how we strive to evade conditions like depression. At the very least, we will treat fear as we do sadness, showing empathy towards individuals experiencing it and seeking to console them.

Likewise, with fear, we won't consider it normal to simply let it be, assuming that fear will vanish once the threat is gone and reappear when a new threat arises, treating it as something commonplace. Instead, we will strive to find ways to overcome fear so that when threats reemerge, the individual in question won't experience fear but will adopt a vigilant stance.

Furthermore, what is even more crucial is taking preventative measures against the emergence of fear or being watchful not to let vigilant attitudes transform into fear. Prevention of the development of fear can only be carried out during childhood by nurturing and habituating children to adopt a **vigilant rather than fearful attitude**.

This can be done by not exposing the child to continuously high-pressure situations, so that the child does not constantly feel threatened. However, it's not feasible for a child to never encounter any form of disturbance, as even the smallest disruption is likely to be analyzed by an individual as a threat.

From as early as 0 years of age, infants automatically or subconsciously sense threats. These threats are more related to internal bodily conditions, such as imbalances in bodily homeostasis like hunger or discomfort. Additionally, there is a sense of discomfort related to external factors, such as the sense of touch on the skin when the infant needs to urinate or have a bowel movement.

As a result, from infancy onward, humans possess an innate vigilance toward uncomfortable or threatening situations, whether they are internal or external to the body. Hence, it requires appropriate parenting, educational approaches, and lifestyle patterns to develop vigilance that is free from the disruptions caused by fear.

Parenting, Education, and Lifestyle Patterns

Parents can contribute to this by ensuring that a child is not consistently placed in psychologically stressful conditions. This is aimed at maintaining the principle of vigilance in infants or children so that it functions optimally and does not transform into fear. The role of parents is to provide **protection** to infants or children, especially when there are **threats** that the child may not be able to handle. This ensures that the parents function as protectors effectively, preventing the child from falling into **fear**.

In reality, many parents often lack an understanding of the things that can pose threats to their children, especially in specific situations. What may be perceived as a non-threatening event or incident by parents can be seen as a threat from a child's perspective. This difference in perception is due to the disparity in age and experience between parents and children, resulting in parents often overlooking these potential threats. Parents tend to be vigilant about threats that align with their own perceptions but may not consider the child's perception of threats, which is based on their cognition, experience, and psychological development.

This situation can lead to children not receiving adequate protection from parents when faced with threats or pressure. In some cases, parents might even add to the pressure the child is facing, viewing the child's response to threats as disruptive or excessive. Alternatively, some parents may downplay or trivialize situations that are threatening to the child.

In certain cases, the parents themselves can become a threat to the child through behaviors like anger. For instance, parents who frequently express anger towards their children and use anger as a method of discipline may inadvertently become a source of threat.

Similarly, in the context of education, the pressure on children needs to be controlled, especially as they reach an age where they can experience stress. This stress can trigger fear in children, and not only in children but also in adults, leading to the development of anxiety disorders.

For adults, it can be quite challenging to measure appropriate levels of pressure to avoid creating stressful conditions. However, in the realm of childhood education, situations that could potentially cause stress can be managed to ensure that children have sufficient awareness that aligns with their cognitive development and needs. This way, the pressure will not lead to the child feeling overwhelmed, stressed, and falling into fear. However, pressure situations at a reasonable level need to be provided to children to train their body's **vigilant** response memory, which is beneficial for them **to adapt** to their environment.

In the subsequent stages of development, when a child enters adolescence, the parenting approach typically changes, and parents can no longer use fear tactics on their child. However, if the pressure continues from parents, adolescents usually tend to resist. The most significant pressure that can influence adolescents often comes from their peer environment.

Adolescents who have a strong foundation of fear due to their upbringing are more prone to feeling pressured and experiencing fear in social situations among peers. These adolescents will struggle to form their own character and tend to conform to social patterns. If such an adolescent associates with "misbehaving" peers, they are likely to engage in similar behavior, and if they associate with "good" peers, they will adopt positive behavior.

Furthermore, a child who is familiar with **fear** is more likely to become a **victim of bullying**, and a child who perceives **anger** as a manifestation of inherited fear is more likely to become a **perpetrator of bullying**. On the other hand, in adolescent children who are not raised with fear, they will adopt a **vigilant and cautious** attitude towards bullying practices. These adolescents won't experience fear, but they will be alert when facing bullying situations, enabling them to think clearly and take necessary actions based on the situation and their cognitive abilities.

Whatever actions these adolescents take, one thing is certain: they will not exhibit signs of fear, whether they choose to confront, defend, or avoid the bullying perpetrator. Not showing fear prevents the bullies' objectives from being achieved, as one of the goals of bullying is to evoke fear and derive satisfaction from the victims' fearful reactions. However, it's important to note that bullying actions can also be related to socio-political, religious, racial, or ethnic differences, and even if victims don't experience fear or anger, they may still be harassed due to such differences. Nevertheless, perpetrators derive greater satisfaction if victims are disturbed and show fear or anger.

Adolescents who do not experience the disturbance of fear are more likely to shape their **own character**, making them psychologically stronger and more confident. They become less susceptible to influence, possess strong convictions, and develop resilience. This outcome arises because their decision-making and experiential learning processes remain unimpeded by fear or anger disruptions.

When these adolescent individuals mature into adults, they are able to make decisions without fear, act more rationally, and, most importantly, they are not easily intimidated or pressured by others or societal systems. One of the most evident examples of distinguishing between individuals who are free from fear yet remain cautious and those who are filled with fear is by observing the development and training of soldiers.

An individual is trained to be vigilant against threats in order to become a skilled soldier. Military training does not aim to make individuals fearful or reckless in the face of danger; instead, it encourages them to exhibit bravery through high levels of vigilance and constant awareness. When these soldiers are deployed to the battlefield, they put into practice the training and simulations they have received.

However, the reality of warfare does not always align with the situations encountered during training or simulations. There are instances where soldiers must improvise to ensure their survival on the battlefield. Sometimes, the pressures faced by soldiers on the battlefield can be extraordinary, creating **highly stressful and life-threatening** conditions that may lead soldiers to experience **war-related trauma**. This shift from a state of **vigilance to fear** can occur due to the immense pressure and life-threatening situations faced by soldiers in combat.

The process of transitioning from vigilance to fear, as explained in the previous section, occurs when the repetitive stress of real combat situations leads to an accumulation of cortisol, thereby diminishing the soldier's ability to think rationally. Soldiers require rational thinking skills because the actual battlefield conditions may differ from training or simulations.

If the situation were exactly the same as in training or simulations, soldiers wouldn't need to rely on rational thinking and could solely rely on the stored body response memory containing vigilance and trained actions. They would be able to handle the pressure, even if it came in succession. However, real-life situations are rarely identical to simulations, so the brain of the soldier will attempt to access the rational part to some extent.

The repeated stress experienced by soldiers on the battlefield causes their rational thinking abilities to decline, replaced by an inability to think clearly under pressure. This state of impaired thinking under pressure, referred to as fear in the previous section, leads the soldier to be dominated by fear, affecting their decision-making abilities.

This fear can develop into trauma if the pressure intensifies or if the soldier experiences events that threaten their safety. The consequence is that soldiers returning from the battlefield may experience **post-traumatic stress disorder (PTSD)**, making them unfit for further assignments. They may even struggle to lead their daily lives and, in some cases, experience suicidal tendencies, not necessarily while they are still on the battlefield, but rather when they attempt to resume their normal civilian lives[56].

The transformation of the principle of alertness or vigilance into fear can also occur in the context of natural disasters or accidents that pose a threat to life and lead someone to experience a near-death experience.

In addition to these two factors, for individuals who are psychologically very healthy, having a normal level of vigilance and not being dominated by fear, the pressures of daily life may not be able to change the principle of vigilance into fear. Unless they find themselves in an extremely high-pressure environment, but with their own awareness, they would likely try to remove themselves from such an environment unless there is no way out, such as civilians trapped in a war zone.

However, it is challenging to find fully psychologically sound adults who have never felt fear since childhood, especially in the current human civilization, which is still caught up in warfare, conflicts, and competition in the struggle to fulfill basic needs and personal ambitions.

Collective mindset or societal opinions to some extent affect an individual's decision-making process, not just the thoughts and opinions of society, but also the systems implemented by the government that play a significant role in influencing an individual's thoughts, including decisions influenced by fear, anxiety, and doubt.

Collective mindset, work patterns, and fear

One of the factors shaping human civilization is the prevailing thoughts in society as well as the civilizational systems developed by authorities and in the current era, by the government. Thoughts that develop generally within society about human development, such as patterns of life development from childhood to adulthood, are also shaped by the government, such as the educational path starting from kindergarten then elementary school, followed by middle school and high school. Then after completing school, pursuing higher education, where the majority of society typically desires to attain a bachelor's degree and then after graduation, seeking employment, often with a strong inclination towards working for the government, getting married, having children, and then the cycle continues.

Such thought patterns are quite common in metropolitan cities in Indonesia, although they may differ in other countries. For instance, in other countries, after graduating from college, a majority of the population might consider starting their own business or becoming experts in a specific field. However, in Indonesia, the desire upon graduation is often to secure a job as an employee, partly due to the large number of public sector job opportunities that were available during the New Order era. This trend has influenced people's perceptions that becoming a civil servant guarantees a stable life, a notion that has shifted more towards working in large private companies post-reformation in 1998 as the government tightened its recruitment of civil servants.

The collective paradigm, understanding, thoughts, and motivations of society at large to some extent influence an individual's ability to make decisions, especially those related to fear. The greater an individual's **foundation of fear** learned through upbringing and education, the more likely they are to make efforts to consistently align with the prevailing mindset of society in general.

Moreover, in Indonesia during the New Order era, especially among government officials, it was highly risky to hold opposing views to the prevailing mainstream mindset at that time, which was tightly controlled by the ruling leaders. There's a saying that goes, "Say something wrong even slightly, and one's career would come to an end, being sent to remote and isolated regions far from centers of power."

These fears, while not as pronounced as during the New Order era, still serve as a general underlying motivation today when seeking employment and earning a livelihood. In Indonesia, very few individuals who have just graduated from college choose not to seek employment for income. Seeking a job has become an ingrained understanding in the general society, especially for adults, particularly men, who are expected to find work and earn a wage. This is because it is what the government provides to accommodate adults in their activities – creating job opportunities, both within the government and in large private companies. Consequently, there's a reluctance or discomfort if not working in a company.

At times, these common beliefs serve as tools for the government to control the population. Even today, some governments still utilize such tactics as a form of propaganda towards their citizens, as seen in North Korea. The Indonesian nation itself requires more time to recover from the indoctrination or propaganda that was carried out during the 32-year New Order era across various domains.

Hierarchy of needs, lifestyle, and fear.

Essentially, in developing countries, the motivation to work, whether as an employee or an entrepreneur, primarily revolves around the goal of earning an income to lead a decent life. Earning income here, of course, refers to acquiring money. If we apply Abraham Maslow's hierarchy of needs, which outlines a hierarchical fulfillment of needs from the most basic to the highest, the basic needs must be met first before progressing to the next level of needs[57].

From the illustration, it can be seen that money can purchase almost all levels of needs except for some basic physical needs such as breathing, excretion, sleep, and the highest level of needs, self-actualization. The rest can be fulfilled by money, and some needs require money to be adequately met, such as proper housing and healthcare, although in Indonesia, there is the BPJS (Social Security Administrator) program that provides more affordable healthcare.

Similarly, in social interactions, social classes are formed based on economic status, which is often indicated by wealth

Picture 2 Hierarchy of Needs

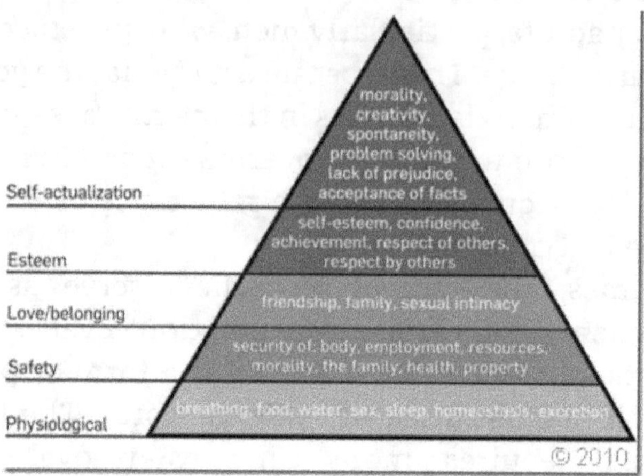

Source
https://id.wikipedia.org/wiki/Berkas:Maslow%27s_Hierarchy_of_
Needs.svg

or money. In terms of the need for recognition, wealth, assets, or money play a significant role in increasing self-esteem, self-confidence, and particularly, many individuals still associate success with the accumulation of wealth and assets.

Regarding self-actualization, generally, the more wealth or assets one possesses, the more opportunities they have for self-actualization. However, there are individuals who strive for self-actualization even without abundant wealth. These individuals can be found in fields related to the arts, like artists, or in creative professions that utilize intellectual capacities, including writers.

Based on the above analysis, in Indonesia, the prevailing perspective is that the primary motivation for adult activities is to earn money. The historical context of the New Order regime has ingrained the idea that earning money through employment, especially as a government employee, is the norm.

Again, different countries have different prevailing perspectives. In developed and prosperous nations, the power of money is not as significant as in developing or third-world countries. Developed countries often provide security and basic needs to their citizens, so not all needs require money. This needs to their citizens, so not all needs require money. This enables citizens to focus on higher-level needs, moving towards self-actualization on Maslow's hierarchy.

People's potential in developed countries tends to be more nurtured than in developing or underdeveloped countries. This is evident in the many influential figures, particularly in the fields of knowledge and society, originating from developed countries in Europe and America from the 1800s to the present.

In general, mainstream thinking, whether in very developed or underdeveloped countries, discourages individuals from thinking differently. This discomfort can even lead to fear in some countries, such as North Korea or Indonesia during the New Order era, especially concerning communist views, which may still evoke fear even today, though not to the same extent as during the New Order.

This situation shows that mass thinking can be controlled by the government or authorities and used as a means of social control. In the post-New Order era, mass thinking is more influenced by economic laws, as money holds significant influence in society. The government's effort to reduce this economic control is aimed at diminishing the wealth gap between the rich and the poor, so that individuals can focus on higher-level needs, just like those who are more financially stable.

Social Change and Fear

Society also plays a significant role in bringing about change and improving well-being. Slowly, individuals can break away from the conventional thinking of meeting basic needs, especially if the government has successfully ensured these needs are met. Even without government intervention, individuals within society can attempt to move beyond conventional thinking and strive to fulfill higher-level needs, particularly those who are financially stable or those willing to take risks despite discomfort.

However, for individuals with a strong foundation of fear due to upbringing or other traumas, breaking away from conventional thinking can be challenging. These individuals can still achieve self-actualization through established pathways or systems formed by prevailing societal norms, depending on the specific situation of the nation and its people.

A notable example in Indonesia is Rio Haryanto, an F1 racing driver who, in 2016, struggled to secure a substantial amount of funding to become an F1 driver, which amounted to 15 million Euros or approximately 225 billion Indonesian Rupiah. Rio's management was able to raise 8 million Euros, and they continued to seek the remaining amount to complete the payment[58]. Such a large amount of money was needed "only for one Indonesian individual" to be able to participate in Formula 1 racing.

Despite their efforts, Rio Haryanto's management ultimately failed to complete the payment within the given deadline, resulting in Rio Haryanto only participating in Formula 1 for half a season[59]. However, this situation at the time sparked pros and cons among the general public, particularly because the funds came from State-Owned Enterprises (BUMN) and were planned to be provided through the Indonesian government. Some members of the public held the opinion that such a large sum of money would be better utilized for other purposes that could benefit the wider population. On the other hand, some people believed that it was justifiable for the government to support Rio Haryanto in order to elevate the nation's pride, as he was representing Indonesia in the prestigious world of Formula 1 racing.

From the perspective of Maslow's hierarchy of needs, the first viewpoint, which considers providing financial assistance as wasteful, is a common thought among those who feel that the country or government is still unable to guarantee the basic needs of its citizens. Meanwhile, the second viewpoint sees Rio Haryanto's presence in Formula 1 as a means to boost national pride, which falls under the category of higher-level needs in the hierarchy.

These differing viewpoints are normal for a developing country striving to become advanced, where a portion of the population is still focused on basic needs, while another portion is starting to consider fulfilling higher-level needs, such as self-esteem. Indonesia's first President, Soekarno, even initiated projects like the National Monument (Monas), which involved significant investment in building Jakarta, despite the economic challenges faced by the newly independent nation. All these efforts were made in pursuit of enhancing national pride[60].

For Rio Haryanto himself, becoming a Formula 1 racer has been a childhood dream. Rio started racing at the age of 6 and has gone through a long journey to reach his current position. Since his early years, Rio has been training to excel in the world of racing. This demonstrates that from a young age, Rio was shaped by his parents to achieve specific goals, which fall under the category of higher-level needs in Maslow's hierarchy, namely the need for self-esteem and pride.

Coming from a relatively well-off economic background, Rio's family did not educate him to focus solely on basic needs. Instead, they nurtured him to achieve success and pursue his dreams in his chosen field, which, in this case, is car racing on the circuit.

Rio's success as a Formula 1 racer has, to some extent, influenced the general mindset of society. It has shown that people shouldn't only focus on meeting their basic needs but can also strive to enhance national pride through individual achievements.

The situation in Indonesia still allows figures like Rio Haryanto to inspire a shift in public thinking towards the fulfillment of self-esteem needs, whether through individual achievements or national pride. However, in less developed countries, especially in economic terms, it can be challenging to achieve this due to the significant prevalence of basic needs issues among the population.

Apart from Rio Haryanto, there is also the name of

Joey Alexander, who at a very young age earned Grammy nominations in the field of music. This further underscores how exceptional individuals can contribute to shaping societal perceptions and aspirations[61]. However, Joey did not create a divide in the public opinion because he did not seek government assistance to achieve his accomplishments.

Another interesting example is Bill Gates and Mark Zuckerberg, who chose to drop out of their university studies to pursue their visionary projects. In this case, Bill Gates founded Microsoft, while Mark Zuckerberg built Facebook[62],[63]. Besides the two of them, there are certainly other individuals who have dropped out of their studies and achieved success.

The decision to leave the world of education to pursue success remains a risk no matter how intelligent the person is, and for Bill Gates, the pressure was even greater than for Mark Zuckerberg because he did it in 1974, not in the modern era[64]. In essence, Bill Gates was indeed very intelligent, but his decision to drop out of college did not align with the common belief that the path to success is primarily through education. After the internet era began, young individuals started leaving their studies and succeeding, as exemplified by Mark Zuckerberg.

However, dropping out or not completing one's education remains a significant issue and is generally viewed as a failure, a burden that risk-takers must bear. Their decision to take this risk depends on the magnitude of their considerations, influenced by their experience of fear. Thinking differently from the mainstream can evoke fear and hinder the ability to think clearly when making independent plans. As a result, many individuals opt to follow the societal norms and existing systems, such as educational and career paths.

This situation leads to a missed opportunity for those who have the potential to develop themselves and their own plans to maximize their potential. They end up wasting their potential for personal growth and the overall advancement of society. This, in turn, encourages the elevation of mainstream thinking to the next level, provided that the government is prepared in various aspects to support the advancement of general thinking in society.

Fundamentally, a nurturing upbringing that fosters alertness rather than fear will enable individuals in society to think clearly. This allows them to independently and accurately position themselves in the societal hierarchy of needs according to their potential. For individuals whose potential is not particularly outstanding, both internally and externally, clear thinking will lead them to follow the societal system and ensure they can meet their basic daily needs.

For those with internal and external potential, clear-mindedness should prompt them to make their own plans, whether through existing societal systems or by devising their own system according to their potential. This enables them to effectively achieve advanced needs, including achieving self-worth through achievements. Such individuals are expected to contribute to human civilization and assist the government in enhancing general societal thinking within the hierarchy of needs.

If successful, they can subtly shift the common mindset in society regarding the need for self-worth and achievement. However, if they fail to achieve their goals, the general societal focus will remain on fulfilling basic needs, dismissing pride and national self-worth as wasteful expenses and efforts.

In order for someone to recognize their own potential and position themselves appropriately in society, the fundamental requirement is to be **free from fear**, especially free from the experiences of fear acquired during childhood. This situation is shaped by parenting patterns, where successful parenting that fosters a healthy **principle of vigilance** will be free from disturbances caused by those principles, namely fear.

In addition to fear, excessive desire or **greed** that makes someone overly bold in taking risks without proper consideration will also keep those individuals trapped in the struggle to fulfill basic needs in the hierarchy of needs pyramid.

Greed itself is a disturbance to the principle of vigilance in facing threats to the principle of pleasure. This topic will be discussed and further explored in the upcoming chapters.

CHAPTER 8
CONCLUSION

It is time to reconfigure the personality structure of Sigmund Freud, particularly focusing on the id located in the subconscious. As explained in Chapter 1, the personality structure introduced by Sigmund Freud consists of the conscious and subconscious minds, depicted using an iceberg model. The conscious mind is like the visible tip of an iceberg, while the vast majority, like the submerged part of an iceberg, lies beneath the surface, representing the subconscious mind.

This iceberg structure comprises three systems: ego, superego, and id. Among these, only ego and superego partially emerge into the conscious, while the id continues to reside in the subconscious. Based on the explanations from earlier chapters, the id undergoes a developmental change in its structure. Previously, it consisted of two drives: the life drive and the death drive. However, it has now evolved into several drives. The first drive is libido, which has expanded beyond its original purpose of reproductive urges. It now extending into the drive for self-development and improvement.

The second aspect involves the drive to self-preservation for as long as possible, based on the principle of homeostasis equilibrium. Lastly, the emergence of threats to libido or the drive for development results in aggression if the libido is threatened, and avoidance behavior if the drive for self-preservation is threatened. These behaviors of aggression and avoidance are referred to as the fight-or-flight instincts.

The libido, the drive for development, operates according to **the pleasure principle**. The drive for self-preservation operates based on **the principle of awareness**. Meanwhile, the drives arising from threats to libido and self-preservation operate based on **the principle of vigilance**.

The division of labor within the id can be separated based on its working principles. Thus, the understanding of the id can be summarized **as fundamental drives that operate based on the principles of pleasure, awareness, and vigilance.**

> **Division of the id:**
> - **Principle of Awareness: Drive for self-preservation.**
> - **Principle of Pleasure: Drive for development.**
> - **Principle of Vigilance: Threats to the principles of awareness and pleasure.**

From this, we can observe that the principles of awareness and pleasure are inherent forms of human drives that work automatically without requiring external stimuli. The principle of awareness prompts humans to automatically monitor bodily homeostasis, while the principle of pleasure drives humans to seek pleasure automatically.

Conversely, the principle of vigilance operates after the presence of external threat stimuli. Humans do not inherently seek threats; although humans may take risks that expose them to threats, behind these risky actions lies the underlying drive to prolong life or to attain pleasure.

Thus, there exists a significant distinction between the principle of vigilance and the other two principles. The principle of vigilance operates when there are threats to both other principles, which can be termed as the principle of vigilance operating when there are threats to the instincts for self-preservation or development.

In conclusion, the principle of vigilance constitutes the fundamental instinct when facing threats. Threats to the instinct of self-preservation trigger caution and avoidance behavior, often referred to as **the instinct to survival**. Threats to the drive for development evoke aggressive actions or "fight," serving as **the instinct to pleasure retention**.

This fundamental instinct when confronting threats, previously known as the death instinct or mortido according to Freud, turns out to be the foundation of aggression observed by Freud. This aggression is rooted in **the vigilant fight-or-flight** response to threats. Consequently, the term mortido, previously associated with the death instinct, transforms into **the instinct to confront threats with vigilance**. Meanwhile, libido, the drive for life, operates not only based on the pleasure principle but also based on the principle of awareness which represents the drive for self-preservation. Hence, the division of the id can be categorized as follows:

- **Libido: Instinct for life**
  - **Principle of awareness:**
    - **Drive for self-preservation**
  - **Principle of pleasure:**
    - **Drive for development**
- **Mortido: Instinct to confront threats**
  - **Principle of vigilance:**
    - **Drive for survival (flight)**
    - **Drive for pleasure retention (fight)**

Within mortido, the drive to save oneself in the form of "flight" can transform into "**fight**", depending on a change in perception from **inferior to superior** towards the threat. Even though the reaction is "fight", the underlying drive remains the preservation of oneself. The same holds for the drive to pleasure retention, which initially takes the form of "fight" but can also change to avoidance or "**flight**", depending on the shift in perception from **superior to inferior** towards the threat.

For libido, **the principle of awareness operates before the principle of pleasure** to ensure that human individuals can survive initially by regulating bodily homeostasis. After achieving a minimum homeostasis balance, the principle of pleasure motivates the fulfillment of individual needs, enabling living beings to grow and develop maximally through meeting physiological and psychological needs.

The principle of pleasure drives living beings to choose more comfortable and enjoyable means to fulfill physiological needs, such as choosing tastier food, more comfortable living spaces, or softer beds. These choices further motivate living beings to consume more food, sleep more soundly and comfortably, fostering maximum growth and activity. Pleasure in sexual relationships also motivates living beings to engage in procreation for the continuation of their species.

An example of the principle of awareness operating before pleasure is human needs for physiological necessities, like food to maintain life, and a place to rest. When humans experience hunger, the principle of awareness prompts them to seek food, and during this search, the principle of pleasure encourages them to choose pleasurable food, such as delicious meals.

However, when food choices are limited, humans will consume whatever sustenance is available, even if it lacks flavor. In this scenario, the pleasure principle either does not operate or operates minimally, focusing on satiating hunger rather than the taste. In cases of extreme hunger, the principle of vigilance takes over, and humans search aggressively for food, consuming it hurriedly.

Similarly, when humans are fatigued, they seek a comfortable bed. However, during severe exhaustion, humans may not choose a comfortable resting place; they might collapse wherever they stand due to fatigue, even losing consciousness. In such circumstances, only the principle of awareness, driven by the body's internal need for rest, operates, without concern for the pleasure principle of finding a comfortable place to rest.

The principle of awareness will shift to the principle of pleasure in the presence of stimulation.
The principle of awareness will transform into the

principle of vigilance when there is a threat to one's safety. The principle of pleasure will turn into the principle of vigilance if there is a threat to pleasure or enjoyment.

In situations where there is no stimulation or threat, the principle of awareness operates to monitor the internal and external conditions of the body to maintain bodily homeostasis. If there is stimulation, the principle of awareness will shift to the principle of pleasure; similarly, if there is a threat, the principle of awareness will shift to the principle of vigilance. The principle of pleasure will also transform into the principle of vigilance if there is a threat while enjoying something, such as food or engaging in enjoyable activities.

The principles of awareness and pleasure are interrelated and inversely proportional. When the principle of awareness is on the rise, the principle of pleasure tends to decrease, and conversely, when the principle of awareness is decreasing, the principle of pleasure tends to increase.

For example, in a situation where the stomach begins to feel hungry, the principle of awareness starts working and informs the mind to search for food. When still in the stage of normal hunger, the individual can still choose foods based on their perception that can provide pleasure, and they select foods that they find delicious.

When the individual is enjoying their meal, the principle of awareness will subside and the pleasure principle will increase. After starting to feel full, the person may begin to feel uncomfortable with the act of eating, and the pleasure principle will decrease while the principle of awareness increases to complete the eating process.

The situation is different when a person is in a state of starvation. In this case, the principle of awareness shifts to the principle of vigilance. The person prioritizes the search for food, and when they find and consume it, the pleasure principle increases, replacing the principle of vigilance. However, if there are other humans or animals attempting to take the food, the vigilance principle will increase again, reducing the pleasure of enjoying the meal. After the eating process, the pleasure principle reverts to the principle of awareness, maintaining the balance of homeostasis.

As long as it doesn't reach overeating, which is usually marked by discomfort in the stomach, the principle of awareness will not shift to vigilance, as it remains within the reasonable tolerance of the body's internal state. However, if vomiting occurs due to overeating, the principle of awareness shifts to vigilance, as this surpasses the body's internal tolerance limit. Similarly, if discomfort due to overeating becomes pronounced, it also crosses the internal tolerance threshold, causing the principle of awareness to shift to vigilance. If this becomes a habit, obesity can occur. "Pleasure brings suffering."

Nevertheless, there are also situations where the pleasure and vigilance principles increase simultaneously, such as in **exciting** circumstances. For instance, facing or attempting to solve a particular mystery creates a sense of excitement.

One of the most classic examples that puzzled Freud was the peek-a-boo game between a mother and a child. Freud was perplexed as to why infants do not develop trauma from this game. The answer lies in the simultaneous increase of the vigilance and pleasure principles. The act of the mother's face disappearing behind her hands increases the child's vigilance, and when her hands are removed, it triggers surprise and joy upon seeing her face. The infant experiences both the vigilance and pleasure principles.

The feelings of excitement and mystery form the foundational basis of human curiosity in acquiring knowledge. This sensation arises from the interplay of the pleasure and vigilance principles. Thus, the peek-a-boo game that puzzled Freud is a form of play that stimulates the infant's curiosity. Eureka...

However, when there are no threats or stimuli, the body operates under the principle of awareness, maintaining a state of stability and **calm**. However, living beings have the innate nature to **reproduce and develop** in order to become better. As a result, the body will automatically generate energy that is ready to be used for growth. When this energy has accumulated, humans will be driven to develop themselves, where the principle of awareness will oversee stimulus responses to attain pleasure.

The principles of vigilance and pleasure move dynamically in an inverse relationship, where the most ideal condition is when both principles are not excessively high or low, avoiding heightened vigilance or pleasure. The balance of homeostasis, which is the function of the principle of awareness, is maintained.

Of course, the principle of vigilance occasionally being in a heightened state is also necessary to enhance human adaptability. This is often implemented by companies aiming to improve an individual's performance, or in military training where the individual is pushed to reach the limits of vigilance while ensuring they do not fall into fear, as explained in the previous chapter regarding fear.

Similarly, the principle of pleasure occasionally being in a heightened state or experiencing great enjoyment in various aspects of life is also essential to enrich life experiences and add variety. This state is often attained when individuals indulge themselves during recreational activities.

However, excessive pleasure can dull an individual's vigilance, reducing their adaptability to unexpected situations. Furthermore, it can lead to various disturbances, particularly if one becomes addicted to pleasure itself, or other disorders like greed, which can result in obesity and other related issues to be discussed further.

Both the principle of vigilance and the principle of

pleasure can experience disturbances that alter their functions, negatively impacting the individual. The principle of vigilance can transform into fear under continuous pressure or turn into anger and frustration in the face of threats to the principle of pleasure. On the other hand, the principle of pleasure itself can escalate into excessive greed and overindulgence, often rooted in disturbances of the principle of vigilance.

We will discuss each of these aspects separately, starting with fear, which can lead to severe mental disorders like schizophrenia—an extreme disruption of the principle of vigilance. We will also explore various other disorders related to the principle of pleasure in the upcoming chapters.

CHAPTER 9
PSYCHOLOGICAL DISORDERS

Every day in their lives, humans always face threats, whether they are threats to their safety or threats that disturb their pleasures. These threats can be real or exist only in their minds. In facing these threats, humans naturally exhibit alertness, which is one of the fundamental instincts known as "mortido."

Mortido, guided by the principle of vigilance, emerges when there is a threat to the drive for self-preservation (the principle of awareness) in the form of the "flight" behavior. It also emerges when there is a threat to the drive for development (the principle of pleasure) in the form of the "fight" behavior.

This principle of vigilance can transform into feelings of **fear** when facing threats to the principle of awareness, or into **anger** when facing threats to the principle of pleasure. **Fear and anger are the most fundamental forms of psychological disturbances**. This is because the natural response to threats is vigilance, which operates based on the **principle of vigilance**.

Thus, the foundation of psychological disturbances lies in the **disruption of mortido**, specifically the disturbance of the principle of vigilance, where alertness in facing threats becomes distorted into feelings of fear or anger. These feelings of fear and anger can then develop into more dangerous psychological disturbances. Therefore, the **death instinct** known as mortido, as discussed in the previous chapter, actually leans more towards the disturbances stemming from mortido itself, where the understanding of mortido has been revised to refer to the instinct in facing threats, and one of its forms of disturbance is the impulse towards death. The following is a further discussion on psychological disturbances, which are disruptions originating from mortido.

Fear and Trauma

The first disturbance of the principle of vigilance we will discuss is extreme fear, known as trauma, which arises from feeling threatened with the loss of life. Intense fear not only becomes a memory in the form of blank thoughts but also manifests as audio-visual events stored in the brain's memory, particularly extreme incidents that endanger the individual's safety.

Recollections of traumatic events, known as trauma memories, often surface in everyday life through dreams or when encountering situations resembling the traumatic event. Traumatic events that pose a greater danger to the individual leave a deeper imprint in their memory. These traumatic events generate energy or force prepared to confront the event. However, if the individual is in a powerless position and unable to escape the event, this energy remains unchanneled. The energy, although strong and meant to be used for survival, becomes trapped.

This trapped energy finds release through dreams, often in the form of nightmares that reenact the traumatic event. The emergence of these nightmares paradoxically generates new energy because the visual imagery in the dream prompts the body to prepare for the danger depicted. However, the new energy that emerges is not as intense as the initial energy of the trauma that is channeled through those dreams. As a result, the memory of the trauma will gradually weaken through the mechanism of these dreams until it completely disappears from the nightmares. But, if the individual continues to encounter events in daily life that reinforce the memory of the trauma, the survival instinct strengthens the trauma, preventing it from fading and keeping it alive within the individual.

As the audio-visual memory of the trauma gradually recedes, what remains is the bodily fear response combined with an overpowering inability to think. This renders the individual more susceptible to potential threatening events, leading to the label of a **timid individual**. As long as the trauma persists, the affected individual will feel inferior in the face of threats related to their trauma, despite being in a superior position compared to the threat in reality.

For instance, an individual who experienced trauma related to cats might feel fearful and inferior when a small domestic cat approaches, even though the person is actually superior to the small cat. However, if the memory of the traumatic event diminishes over time or through therapy to address the trauma, what remains is only the memory of the bodily fear response to the traumatic event. In this position, the individual can choose to remain inferior, act superior, or adopt the most effective approach: **rational thinking**. Opting for an inferior stance may lead the individual to flee without considering why or what prompted their flight.

Choosing rational thinking allows the individual to react by fleeing while contemplating why they are doing so and what exactly triggers their fear. If their rational thinking is sound, they can better control their reactions to the threat, gradually reducing the excessive response, and over time, the fear may dissipate. Nonetheless, a slight reaction will persist as a form of vigilance due to the enduring bodily response stored in the amygdala.

If the individual decides to adopt a superior stance towards the threat, they will react aggressively to eliminate it, which is known as anger. Anger culminates in a sense of satisfaction after expressing it, as **anger is a disturbance of the**

principle of vigilance in response to the principle of pleasure.

Another case examined by Freud involves traumatized soldiers from World War I, in which he concluded the presence of a death instinct. These soldiers continuously recall the traumatic event due to a lack of resolution when confronting the threat, causing a blank mental state. Traumatized individuals' recollection of bad experiences is not because of a death instinct, but because the energy that remained unchanneled during the traumatic event is still present within their bodies. This powerful energy becomes attached to the audio-visual memory. Ideally, this energy should diminish through natural mechanisms like bad dreams. However, many soldiers returning from war zones lack adequate psychological support in their daily lives. Consequently, instead of recovering, they struggle to adapt, worsening their psychological condition. The trauma they carry can evolve into depression.

Depression

The next psychological disorder is when fear is constantly repressed, unable to be channeled, and the individual remains fixated on the internal fears, leading to depression.

Depression arises from a loss of hope in leading one's life. This situation originates from excessive fear, wherein the overwhelming sense of inferiority and low self-worth results in feeling trapped, isolated, and significantly reduces activities. This limits exploration of life due to the multitude of fears. This situation creates a feeling of having no options in life, making life seem narrow, and energy is constrained within. The energy that arises from fear, the energy generated by pressures that cannot be released, can turn inward and potentially lead to suicidal tendencies due to depression.

Apart from fear related to various aspects, depression can also be caused by events that make one perceive a loss of something valuable in their life, in accordance with their ideals or what is valuable to their superego.

In this condition, depression often occurs in individuals who have experienced sexual violence, job loss, or the loss of loved ones. The pressure leading to the loss of these ideals is typically accompanied by fear and a loss of clear thinking due to blank thoughts.

Trauma conditions that nearly extinguish one's life are also highly susceptible to falling into depression, as mentioned earlier. It is crucial to maintain the psychological state of individuals who have experienced trauma, assisting them to adapt and gradually overcome their trauma, allowing their energy to flow through nightmares. It's essential to avoid falling into a state of depression that could cause the traumatic energy to rebound and drive them toward death. This death drive, as observed by Freud, is actually a **disturbance of mortido**, a disturbance of the **principle of vigilance**, a principle in facing threats.

Anxiety

As human perception evolves, individuals become capable of predicting the future, including potential future threats. Some respond with vigilance, while others react with fear when faced with uncertain future events that threaten their safety.

Anxiety is a form of fear related to uncertain future events. While children easily experience fear, adults tend to feel anxious. Children often fear their fantasies, whereas adults often fear an uncertain future. Anxiety can be described as a mature version of fear; the difference lies in perceptual abilities. Adults possess a higher capacity to predict the future, leading to fear of the unknown future or events that may never transpire, which is known as **anxiety**.

From this anxiety, various other forms of psychological disorders often develop, especially in the form of **dependencies**. If not experiencing dependency, untreated anxiety can develop into more severe forms of psychological disorders.

The most effective way to deal with anxiety is to

investigate its root cause, which often originates from fear. Accumulated fear from childhood or past traumas usually forms the roots of anxiety. By transforming this fear back into a sense of vigilance, individuals can become vigilance to uncertainties related to the future.

Anger and Frustation

Humans, from infancy, have their basic minimum needs for self-preservation fulfilled. When babies are not hungry, thirsty, hot, or cold, their subsequent activities are driven by developmental impulses such as enjoying food, playing, and engaging in other pleasurable activities.

The purpose of these activities is to gain pleasure or enjoyment based on the principle of pleasure. When this pleasure or enjoyment is disrupted, the baby will cry. For instance, if a baby is breastfeeding and is suddenly pulled away, the baby will cry. Similarly, if a baby has developed a habit of sucking on a pacifier and the pacifier is taken away, the baby will cry. In this context, crying can be interpreted as a form of aggressive crying, a response to a threat to pleasure or enjoyment.

Aggressive crying is different from crying due to a threat to one's safety, which is referred to as "avoidant" crying. Both conditions of crying should be distinguishable by parents. If left unchecked, aggressive crying can lead to feelings of **anger,** while crying due to a threat to safety can lead to feelings of **fear**. Aggressive crying is a **"fight"** response in infants, while crying to "avoid" is a **"flight"** response in infants to a threat.

Of course, just like fear, infants and children can also easily become angry when facing threats to their pleasures. Thus, the role of parents is crucial in maintaining a vigilant state in children to prevent them from easily falling into anger. Because if not taken care of, this could develop into a tendency to easily become frustrated as adults when facing challenges in realizing their desires, or they may easily become angry if their pleasures are disrupted. The appropriate attitude is to be **aggressively vigilant** when facing challenges or threats to pleasure and enjoyment.

Similar to fear, continuous threats to pleasure in adults can also lead to feelings of anger, where the sense of be aggressive vigilance is lost. Expressing aggression is a natural response when there is a threat to the principle of pleasure, but if this aggression is not accompanied by clear thinking or results in "going blank," it's referred to as anger. Anger is certainly not as effective as the attitude of aggressive vigilance, which still allows for clear thinking.

Similarly to anxiety related to uncertainty about the future, **frustration** is caused by anger towards uncertain circumstances. Frustration leads to accumulated angry energy, for example, a mother might become frustrated because her child is struggling to understand the given lessons, a man might become frustrated due to his lack of success in pursuing a desired woman. The aggression of anger can become increasingly dangerous and often results in harmful aggressive actions.

In simple terms, anxiety is the fear of uncertainty about self-preservation, while **frustration is the anger of uncertainty** about achieving desires. Self-preservation is the drive to stay alive, while fulfilling desires is the drive to develop.

If this sense of frustration is left unchecked, it can gradually lead to hysteria, impatience, difficulty in self-control regarding aggressive actions, loss of clear thinking ability, and may eventually lead to more severe psychological disorders. And most importantly, the most damaging aspect is when frustration evolves into the form of **greed**.

Individuals who are trapped in frustration will lose their patience in achieving their desires. However, instead of giving up, they tend to develop a greedy attitude towards what they want. Anxiety makes people easily give up and become desperate when facing obstacles. Frustration will make people more aggressive and daring to violate all ethics, morals, and rules to obtain their desires.

Conflict

Human beings inevitably experience conflicts in their lives. Conflicts among individuals are natural; it is impossible for humans to avoid conflicts entirely. Conflicts, within certain limits, are necessary to enhance human adaptability.

Essentially, conflicts between individuals can occur when the threatened individual does not adopt an inferior stance towards the threatening individual. In such cases, both individuals will compete for a superior position, and the winner will take the superior position while the loser will end up in an inferior position.

Conflicts that remain within the bounds of reason, in the pursuit of a superior position, are based on vigilance accompanied by clear thinking. Conflicts become uncontrollable and highly destructive when driven by anger in the pursuit of a superior position, with the intention of making the opposing party feel afraid.

The pressure of anger is not as strong as the pressure of fear. This difference in pressure arises because in the position of anger, there is still a possibility to neutralize the threat with aggressive behavior based on superiority. However, if one fails to maintain their superiority, they will become inferior and fall into a state of fear, where the pressure will increase. In a state of inferiority, one can no longer attempt to assert superiority but instead focuses on their own safety while overwhelmed by fear and dulled thinking.

Consequently, both parties will stubbornly use their anger to gain a superior position. For the loser, this can have fatal consequences, ranging from trauma to even loss of life.

Healthy conflict, based on vigilance, aims to compete for a superior position but prioritizes mutual understanding over unilateral victory. The ability to understand each other will be lost if trapped by fear and anger, where **winning** becomes the sole focus.

Insanity Originating from Nightmares

Next is a psychological disorder stemming from fear that begins with nightmares, anxiety, delusions, false beliefs, and hallucinations, leading to a more severe disorder, schizophrenia. Fear-related disorders can manifest as nightmares during sleep at night. Dreams serve the function of releasing built-up energy that has not been discharged while the individual is awake.

The simplest example is unmet sexual needs in wakeful consciousness, which may be fulfilled in dreams. Not only sexual needs but also unfulfilled sexual desires in wakeful consciousness can find fulfillment in dreams. Additionally, the need for releasing pressure from suppressed vigilance principles that cannot be discharged in wakeful consciousness is also channeled through dreams, resulting in nightmares. If the fulfillment of sexual needs gives rise to pleasant dreams, **the release of pressure needs may lead to nightmares**.

Nightmares are actually a form of natural therapy for releasing pent-up pressure from psychological disorders, such as fear-induced stress or trauma. These pressures cannot be expressed and remain suppressed in the subconscious, eventually emerging in the form of nightmares. The greater the level of fear or stress experienced, the more intense the nightmares become.

Of course, this phenomenon has been known for a long time, as evidenced by the dream analysis theory developed by Sigmund Freud[65]. Then Joe Griffin, a psychologist from Ireland, further developed the concept of pressure being channeled through dreams. He explained that individuals experiencing depression tend to have more frequent dreams compared to those who are not depressed.

One significant explanation provided by Joe Griffin is that all psychological disorders, ranging from anxiety, anger, depression, and culminating in psychotic disorders like delusions, hallucinations, and ultimately insanity, form a **continuum** that begins from a normal human state and progresses to the psychotic stage[66].

The pressures that initially create fear, and if they continue to develop into depression, will make the nightmares they experience worse. Furthermore, as perceptions increasingly influence the state of distress they are experiencing, delusions or false beliefs about reality begin to emerge. **These delusions** are, in fact, a form of channeling through rationality, but with foundations of belief influenced by the pressures stemming from anxiety or frustration.

The most prevalent example is in cases of terrorism, where these delusion are exploited as outlets for the pressures existing in the subconscious. It's easier to recruit individuals experiencing high levels of stress than to recruit psychologically healthy individuals to join terrorists[67].

After delusions, the pressures experienced by the individual will intensify because living with delusions makes it increasingly difficult for the individual to adapt, leading to more stress and problems. As a result, these delusions will be reinforced by very high levels of anxiety and frustration, further worsening the quality of their dreams.

Subsequently, another disturbance begins to occur: the dream world starts **to infiltrate** the conscious realm, manifesting as voices, whispers, and erroneous visualizations accompanied by false beliefs. This process is known as **hallucination**. The culmination of this disturbance is when the dream world continues to persist even after the individual has awakened or become conscious, placing them in a realm of imagination where they are unable to connect with the ordinary reality we call insanity or schizophrenia. **Insanity is a nightmare that becomes reality**.

Dreams initially only occur when the individual is asleep, but as life's pressures increase, dreams during sleep may not suffice to release the pent-up stress. Consequently, even when awake, nightmares persist as a means of channeling overwhelming stress.

In essence, dreams serve as a natural form of therapy. When an individual is under pressure or stress, they channel this pressure through bad dreams, although not all the stress can be released at once. This depends greatly on the magnitude of the individual's stress.

Therefore, individuals experiencing mild stress can recover by resting for a few days and allowing dreams to serve as a natural therapy to alleviate the stress. During this period, the individual must be completely free from any mental burdens, in a state of true relaxation and ease.

The simplest function of mental hospitals is to prevent patients from experiencing further life pressures and to facilitate the most basic form of natural therapy: allowing dreams to alleviate life pressures. This occurs both when the patient is conscious and while they sleep. The hope is that over time, the frequency of distressing dreams will decrease, allowing the patient to interact with reality once more. This condition signifies that the patient is starting to reintegrate with reality.

Of course, in order to lead a life free from additional stress, patients need assistance from nurses who ensure they do not encounter further life pressures. If a patient enters a mental hospital or any rehabilitation center and finds their life pressures increasing, it could be said that the institution has **failed** to fulfill its fundamental function of reducing life pressures for the patient.

Dependency

Dependency is a way for humans to alleviate anxiety and frustration by channeling the energy arising from anxiety or frustration into the pursuit of pleasure based on the operation of the **pleasure principle**. However, this channeling will not completely eliminate anxiety and frustration, only temporarily reduce them, and they will resurface later. Forms of dependency are numerous, ranging from smoking, gaming, food, drugs, sex, to material possessions and money.

Dependency indeed can help manage anxiety and frustration from developing into more severe psychological disorders. However, due to this dependency, individuals become more susceptible to being controlled by others, especially when it concerns money. Money can buy various forms of dependency as "anxiety-relieving" remedies. As a result, human life's true motivations shift from the drive for self-preservation and development to anxiety and frustration.

Yes, that's correct. Human motivation nowadays is largely based on anxiety and frustration. To prevent these from causing harm, various forms of dependency are provided to alleviate anxiety and frustration, particularly in the form of money, which allows individuals to purchase their "dependency drugs."

Certainly, as the human brain develops, the relationship between anxiety and frustration becomes more dynamic. Similar to the relationship between fear and anger, anxiety can transform into frustration and vice versa. The forms of these "dependency drugs" will also become more complex. Humans are intelligent beings, but they are also susceptible to falling into psychological disorders.

Forms of dependence based on Maslow's hierarchy of needs

As explained earlier, fear can develop into more severe disorders or transform into anger as perceptions shift from inferiority to superiority. This anger can further evolve into frustration when facing uncertainty in achieving desires.
When fear transforms into anger, the energy that once originated from fear can be channeled through anger. In addition to anger, fear can also be channeled through various forms of dependency to alleviate fear, especially when fear has evolved into more complex anxieties. The channeling in the form of **dependency** operates based on the **pleasure principle**.

Dependency in basic needs, for instance, such as the need

Picture 2 Hierarchy of Needs

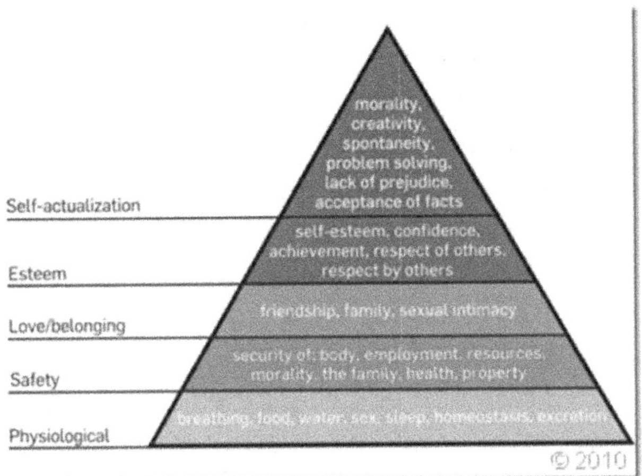

Source:
https://id.wikipedia.org/wiki/Berkas:Maslow%27s_Hierarchy_of_
Needs.svg

for food, can manifest as gluttony. Then, at an advanced level, the need for a sense of security will emerge, represented by ownership, namely a home, employment for income, health, and family well-being, where these needs can be met if the individual possesses sufficient wealth.

In healthy individuals, these needs will be pursued minimally to ensure a decent life in accordance with the awareness principle, and efforts will be made to enhance them for a comfortable life in line with the pleasure principle. However, much like overindulgence in eating, the same applies to individuals with a background of strong anxiety or frustration. They too will lose the ability to think logically and rationally in their endeavor to fulfill their needs for a sense of security.

In the human endeavor to meet the need for security, which is the second need after physiological needs, individuals with psychological disorders rooted in intense fear and anxiety, such as depression, will face difficulties in satisfying these needs. They may lack motivation, lose focus, easily give up, feel weak, become lazy, and so on, as they become preoccupied feel weak, become lazy, and so on, as they become preoccupied and exhausted by their own fears and anxieties, depleting their energy and strength to strive for fulfillment.

The worse their condition becomes, the harder it is for them to meet their life needs. In the most severe cases, they may be unable to fulfill even their basic physiological needs, such as eating, drinking, and bathing, as seen in people with schizophrenia.

On the other hand, individuals who can channel their pressure through dependencies based on the **pleasure principle**, apart from anger and unhealthy dependencies like excessive sexual activity and overeating, can channel it through determined efforts to fulfill their needs, especially the need for security. According to these individuals, who are driven by fear, anxiety, or frustration, meeting their need for security—such as ownership of property, employment, housing, income, and all things related to wealth or money—can free them from fear. They believe that obtaining these things will provide them with a sense of security.

The individual will strive tirelessly to accumulate money and wealth in order to purchase a sense of security. With hard work, proficiency, and a good understanding of applicable laws, they can become very wealthy. However, if they lack a good understanding of the law and fail to consider the consequences of their actions on others, they may be inclined to break the law in order to amass wealth. This can range from white-collar crimes like corruption to criminal acts such as robbery and theft.

Individuals trapped in the cycle of dependency through relentless efforts to achieve a sense of security, whether through lawful or unlawful means, will **never feel satisfied** with the wealth they acquire. The individual will never be able to buy a sense of security to eliminate fear, anxiety, or frustration, as these feelings remain stored in their memory, haunting them continuously.

The sense of security in a healthy individual is not meant

to erase fear, anxiety, and frustration, but rather **to fulfill the principle of awareness**, allowing humans to live decently. This then evolves into the motivation of the **pleasure principle**, driving the individual to strive for a comfortable life. The comfort experienced by humans is rooted in the motivation of the pleasure principle, so once they feel comfortable, they can move on to fulfilling their next life needs, such as the need for **love and companionship**.

Meanwhile, for individuals motivated by fear, anxiety, or frustration, they will remain trapped in the need for security and continue accumulating wealth, whether through legitimate or illegitimate means. They will never be able to enjoy their wealth because their motivation is solely to channel their fear, anxiety, or frustration through the pleasure principle, rather than for self-development. As a result, these individuals become dependent on material wealth.

So, the dependence on material wealth is driven by two motivations: the fear of poverty and the desire for quick wealth due to frustration. Simply put, it can be termed **as fear of poverty and greed**.

Greed or the fear of poverty ensnares the individual in the trap of material possessions, wealth, and money. The individual believes that not only a sense of security can be bought with money, but also subsequent needs like the need for love and companionship, self-esteem, and even self-actualization can be purchased with money. This further entrenches them in a **dependence on material wealth**.

The connection between friendship and love is evaluated based on money, then self-esteem is judged by wealth, and finally self-actualization, including morality, is also attempted to be bought with money. This has led to the emergence of a societal idiom that states that justice favors the wealthy. Unfortunately, even if an individual is able to purchase morality, including justice in this case, they will still live in the shadows of fear and frustration – the fear that their kingdom will collapse.

Dependency on material wealth forms a vicious cycle of

fearing loss, becoming greedy, fearing loss again, and so on. This creates a cycle of fear – greed – fear – greed, trapping the individual in a cycle of misery without being able to truly experience and enjoy life.

Individuals trapped in this pattern of dependence are actually ensnared in the need for security in Maslow's hierarchy, and they will never be able to progress to fulfilling their higher-level needs.

Possessiveness and Obsession

This recurring pattern of dependence is not only related to material wealth. This dependency disorder can also be associated with love, which is initially based on the principle of pleasure. However, this principle of pleasure in love can transform into a form of dependence when intervened by fear, thus turning love into possessiveness – the fear of losing one's partner – or even into obsession, driven by excessive desire rooted in frustration, the desire to quickly attain the desired person.

Possessiveness and obsession towards someone can then transform into hatred. This energy of hatred actually originates from the energy of love that transforms into the energy of desire – desire that is fueled by lust – and then transforms again into the energy of hatred, evolving into the energy of anger. The shift from possessiveness and obsession to hatred is certainly connected to the unfulfilled nature of the possessive and obsessive feelings held by the individual. These feelings cannot be satisfied because they are rooted in fear and frustration.

The failure to satisfy the principle of pleasure leaves a person with two choices: to blame themselves or to blame their partner. If they blame themselves, the individual will experience added fear in forming new relationships with others and will begin to blame themselves.

On the other hand, if they blame their partner for the unfulfilled satisfaction of their possessive and obsessive feelings, the individual may develop hatred towards their partner and potentially channel their wrathful impulses into a form of animosity towards them.

The Trap of Capitalism

Essentially, the disturbance of the vigilance principle towards the principles of awareness and pleasure leads to anxiety and frustration, caused by instances of blank memory that then form habits into a pattern of life, namely a life shrouded in anxiety and frustration, resulting in feelings of fear of poverty and greed.

Unfortunately, the current system forms a pattern of dependency on wealth through anxiety and frustration, fueling the capitalist or free market system, where the rich get richer and the poor get poorer. The capitalist system is built upon the fears and greed for money, the fear of not having enough and the greed to have as much money as possible.

Ironically, it's quite amusing to call it a "free market" because the market that emerges is not truly free, but rather controlled by a privileged few who hold power over it. In Indonesia, there is a considerable effort by the government to avoid getting trapped in the free market, but, of course, the citizens themselves must break free from fear and greed in order to truly achieve economic independence and freedom.

Freud extensively explained the principle of pleasure through libido, a theory exploited by marketing professionals to offer the pleasures of their products to the public, ultimately leading to the understanding that being wealthy is immensely pleasurable, and all forms of libido or pleasure can be channeled through wealth.

Society competes fervently to become wealthy, striving to accumulate money by any means, whether legitimate or illegitimate. On the other hand, fear has become a common aspect in society, especially the fear of not having money, given the immense power that money wields in this system.

Generally, society still considers fear as something normal or inherent, which is why parenting and education approaches that may induce fear are still prevalent, despite ongoing campaigns against violence towards children. Progress has been made towards a better understanding of nonviolent parenting, rooted in anger-free approaches, However, it has not yet reached an understanding of **the dangers of fear**.

Previous generations of individuals who have been raised with violence and have a significant level of fear, as adults, carry enough fear to prevent them from reaching the advanced levels of need fulfillment in Maslow's hierarchy. Instead, they will continuously focus on accumulating wealth, which will never be sufficient to fulfill the highest-level needs, such as self-esteem, and they will likely never achieve self-actualization.

For the capitalist system, it is crucial that these individuals remain controlled by fear and greed. Through instilling fear and greed, individuals are compelled to work hard to accumulate money to alleviate their fears, and then they spend that money to satisfy their greed. This situation indirectly forms a vicious cycle, where society works tirelessly to produce more and more goods. They then consume these goods in excessive amounts, never feeling content or satisfied. This situation leads to a constant increase in production as the global population grows, driven by escalating fear and greed gripping the society.

Human civilization no longer revolves around fulfilling genuine needs but is dictated by the insatiable appetite for greed. In this scenario, the most affected entity is our beloved planet, Earth. Excessive production damages the Earth's natural environment. For instance, consider the rampant forest fires in Sumatra and Kalimantan due to the greed of palm oil plantation companies eager to maximize production without regard for environmental destruction.

If our planet is damaged beyond repair, human civilization itself will be threatened, and the story of humanity could come to an end due to the fear and greed exploited by the capitalist system. Before we delve further into the system that fosters fear and greed in humans, let's explore the principle of awareness in the next chapter.

CHAPTER 10
AWARENESS

What is the principle of awareness actually, has no one researched it before, and what about its position within the libido which is a part of the basic instinct deep within the human subconscious? In 2014, Scarlett Johansson, who is one of my favorite actresses, portrayed a character named Lucy in a film titled the same as her character, Lucy.

I won't delve into the discussion about the notion that humans only use 10% of their brain, and if they could use 100%, they could become superhuman[68], That's not interesting to me. However, there's one intriguing statement from Professor Norman, portrayed by Morgan Freeman, regarding immortality vs. reproduction, and here's the quote:

"For primitive beings like us, life seems to have only one single purpose: gaining time. And it is going through time that seems to be also the only real purpose of each of the cells in our bodies. To achieve that aim, the mass of the cells that make up earthworms and human beings has only two solutions. Be immortal, or to reproduce. If its habitat is not sufficiently favorable or nurturing, the cell will choose immortality. In other words, self-sufficiency and self-management. On the other hand, if the habitat is favorable, they will choose to reproduce. That way, when they die, they hand down essential information and knowledge to the next cell. Which hands it down to the next cell and so on. Thus knowledge and learning are handed down through time"[69].

I won't discuss whether I agree or disagree with the quote above, but what's interesting is the choice between **"be immortal, or to reproduce."**. We all know that reproduction works based on the pleasure principle, so does immortality then mean utilizing the awareness principle? We're also aware that humans, if given the choice, would desire to live forever, and the concept of immortality has become an intriguing topic. Does this suggest that the desire for immortality exists within every human?

The above quote indicates that cells choose between immortality or reproduction. However, if this isn't a choice but rather a natural drive within humans for both immortality and reproduction, then these drives for eternal life and reproduction are best suited to reside in the subconscious, in the id, the most fundamental instinct of humans.

In the movie "Lucy," it's stated that cells will choose between immortality and reproduction. Let's reinterpret this: immortality and reproduction aren't choices, but rather primal drives that both exist within the id, in the form of libido. The distinction is that in a choice, one of these options would disappear – if immortality is chosen, reproduction would vanish, and vice versa. However, as primal drives within the id in the form of libido, both these drives persist – the drive for immortality and the drive for reproduction. Thus, the awareness principle encompasses not only the drive for self-preservation but also the drive for eternal life.

We are very familiar with the primal drive for reproduction, and we also understand the desire for immortality, yet we haven't fully grasped that the urge or desire for immortality is itself a primal drive. Let's delve deeper and explore its implications for human civilization.

The drive for eternal life has, up until now, remained unrealized by humans since no human has achieved immortality. In reality, humans continue to experience sadness at the death of their loved ones and worry about their own mortality.

The presence of an unattainable drive for eternal life, which cannot be realized during human life, has led human civilization to develop understanding and thoughts, manifested through the proliferation of ideas about life after death. These ideas serve as a significant indication that humans indeed possess a drive or desire to persist eternally.

The most common concept is the existence of heaven after death, where humans will live eternally in a place devoid of suffering, and they will perpetually experience joy and happiness. On the contrary, there's the concept of hell, where humans will suffer eternally. Additionally, there's the concept of reincarnation, where humans, after death, are reborn not only as humans but also as other living beings. The concept of salvation through physical bodily resurrection is also prevalent among Christians' beliefs in eternal life.

However, the desire or drive for eternal life can be disrupted, particularly by the fear of death. The psychologically healthiest attitude when death approaches is acceptance since it's inevitable. This indicates that the individual is not afflicted by the fear of death. The uncertainty about what occurs after death burdens the awareness principle, which always seeks to reduce uncertainty in order to prolong life. Logic and thought are yet to offer definitive answers and can only provide conjectures, not facts.

The fear of death emerges when the individual is unable to think clearly, similar to other fears caused by instances of blank memory. The individual becomes incapable of processing the fact that they don't know what happens after death, leading to constant restlessness and futile attempts to guess until death arrives. Concepts about life after death arise from the drive for immortality and the fear of death itself. These concepts seemingly aim to provide certainty to the awareness principle, reassuring the individual of eternal life through suggestions and convictions.

For psychologically healthy individuals, they don't dwell excessively on suggestions or justifications regarding what occurs after death; they simply adopt a passive attitude. On the other hand, individuals plagued by the fear of death become frightened and strive to find answers using logic, even though they may never succeed. Meanwhile, individuals who possess a strong belief and successfully self-suggest or rationalize using their logic, and are deeply convinced about what will happen to them after death, will not fear facing death, as long as they continue to engage in repetitive suggestions or logical justifications until their final moments.

Suicide bombers continuously receive such suggestions, eliminating their fear of death. A well-known phrase in Indonesia, "accompanied by 72 heavenly virgins," is often expressed by terrorists who carry out suicide bombings[70].

The drive for immortal life and the disturbance of the fear of death have given rise to concepts of life after death, spanning from prehistoric times with beliefs in ancestral spirits residing in trees or sacred mountains, to the development of religions with concepts of heaven and hell, or the concept of reincarnation. This demonstrates that the subconscious drive for immortality strives to manifest itself in the conscious mind through conscious thoughts, resulting in these concepts.

Meanwhile, in the subconscious realm, the desire for immortality is represented by the awareness principle, which continuously monitors the body's homeostatic balance to ensure it remains stable, with the goal of enabling the body to survive or live as long as possible.

However, our exploration does not stop here. I will delve further into this awareness principle and explore to what extent the fundamental instinct of the drive for immortality influences human life.

I will discuss one of the most intriguing stories on Earth, the story of Buddha, the tale of Siddhartha Gautama. This story is particularly relevant for delving into the awareness principle. Deepak Chopra, an alternative medicine practitioner and spiritual author, beautifully recounts the journey of Prince Siddhartha to becoming Buddha in his novel "Buddha"[71]. I will extract the essence of Buddha's story from this novel and additional references.

Roughly in the 6th century BCE, a Prince was born named Siddhartha Gautama. Siddhartha's early life was closely intertwined with the prophecies of ascetics led by Asita Kaladewala, who predicted that Siddhartha could either become a King or even a Buddha.

This prophecy left King Suddhodana, the father of Prince Siddhartha, restless, as he desired his son to become a King rather than a Buddha. The condition set by the ascetics to prevent Siddhartha from becoming a Buddha was that he must avoid encountering four specific events: an old person, a sick person, a dead person, and an ascetic[72].

The prophecy led King Suddhodana to confine his son within the palace and create a palace resembling heaven for Siddhartha. In this palace, there was no suffering or hardship; only joy and luxury prevailed[73].

Throughout his childhood to becoming a Buddha, Prince Siddhartha was often tempted by Mara, the demon king, who sought to control Siddhartha through both sensual temptations and fear. However, Mara was unable to conquer Siddhartha's mind and continued his attempts[74].

After reaching adulthood, Siddhartha Gautama, at the age of 29, left his palace and encountered his people. Upon seeing his subjects, the Prince was shocked to witness sickness, death, and suffering among them[75]. After that, with a sense of curiosity,

Siddhartha began to contemplate why people experience sickness, aging, and suffering. His contemplation led him through various ascetic adventures, where he encountered various temptations and threats posed by Mara.

The Ascetic Gautama successfully navigated through temptations, threats, physical pain, and fears of torment, enduring everything without wavering in his meditation. He even reached the gates of Hell, but he was turned away because no sin was found within him. However, the Ascetic Gautama chose to enter the gates of Hell and endure all the torments it offered. He underwent the torments continuously as if they were routines, and this repetitive cycle eventually bored his mind. The torments aimed at causing harm and instilling fear had no effect on Gautama. Despite his bones breaking and his skin tearing, he would heal every morning, only to be tormented again the next day. This monotonous routine left Gautama feeling bored.

Eventually, the vision of Hell disappeared, and the Ascetic Gautama realized that he had overcome all forms of suffering he could imagine. With his body no longer feeling any pain and his mind no longer responding to desires, he made the decision to open his eyes[76].

As he began to regain his bodily sensations, the Ascetic Gautama realized that his body had become extremely weak, and he felt incredibly thirsty. Doubt crept into his mind about whether he would survive. Lying weak and helpless, a young girl approached him and offered him food.

During his recovery process, Siddhartha felt that he had failed to achieve complete enlightenment, and he now had no desires or concerns. Once his condition improved, the Ascetic Gautama was unsure of what to do next. Should he return home and become a king, or should he seek a livelihood to live independently, detached from his previous occupation? He felt a sense of emptiness and hollowness, like vapor, unable to make a choice.

As he walked, the Ascetic Gautama felt like he was moving automatically, and his body seemed transparent. He observed the natural scenery and felt each sensation penetrating his body. "I am water," he thought. "I am air." The Ascetic Gautama became somewhat certain that he had transformed into something new, a human who was not quite human.

Then, he encountered a tall tree and sat beneath it to meditate. He pondered whether a person who felt hollow needed to meditate. Initially, the answer was no. But because he didn't know what to do and where to go, he decided to meditate, gazing at the moon. Gautama thought about how wonderful it would be to become the moon. And then, it happened[77].

After seven weeks had passed, during which the Ascetic Gautama enjoyed the moon, Mara returned once again, offering all his knowledge and wisdom about life and the universe to satisfy Gautama's curiosity. However, the Ascetic Gautama declined Mara's offer with the response, "One who wishes to know everything no longer exists, and there is nothing more I wish to ask." And finally,

Mara unleashed his ultimate weapon – his three beautiful daughters – to tempt the Ascetic Gautama into accepting them as wives.

The first daughter was named Tanha, meaning desire. Gautama spoke, "Your name means 'desire.' I will take you as my wife, but alas, I have no desire for you. If you marry me, you will never experience desire, and no one will desire you. Can you accept this?" The first daughter of Mara became furious and revealed a face with long fangs, growling before departing.

Next came the second daughter, Raga, meaning lust. Like with the first, Gautama said, "I will take you as my wife, but your heart, made of fire, will freeze, and you will never feel lust, and no one will lust after you. Can you accept this?" Raga became angry and transformed into a ball of fire, attempting to engulf Gautama, yet the flames vanished before him and disappeared.

Then, the youngest daughter of Mara arrived, named Arati, meaning aversion. Gautama spoke, "You desire nothing because you abhor everything. I will make you my wife, but only if you open yourself to love. Can you accept this?" Hearing this, Arati felt an immense disgust, and in an instant, she vanished like her two older sisters[78].

Witnessing his three daughters depart, Mara became furious. However, Mara couldn't challenge Gautama, as Gautama admitted that he no longer had a soul, and only those with a soul could be cursed. Of course, Mara didn't believe this and accused Gautama of madness, as Mara was convinced that all beings possessed souls. Gautama then challenged Mara to prove it for himself – if Mara could find Gautama's soul, it would belong to Mara. Meanwhile, Gautama remained indifferent to the matter.

Mara went off in search of Gautama's soul, contemplating whether Gautama had a soul or not. Gautama himself didn't care if he had a soul or not, and he was no longer attached to his soul.

Once Mara had left, the Ascetic Gautama resumed his enjoyment of being the moon, understanding that he needed to be empty, bare. Only in this innocence could his mask be removed. "So, this is it," Gautama thought. "The truth." He had attained his freedom, and within that freedom, anything was possible[79].

A very interesting story indeed, and there is one particularly intriguing aspect that many people tend to overlook while focusing more on how Ascetic Gautama achieved enlightenment. This intriguing element pertains to **the upbringing** provided by King Suddhodana to his son, Siddhartha Gautama.

As we are aware from the narrative above, King Suddhodana raised his son in an environment filled with joy, where Siddhartha Gautama was shielded from sorrow, suffering, and any form of hardship until the age of 29, when he finally ventured out of the palace and witnessed suffering for the first time.

The nurturing provided by the King to his Prince demonstrates that from a young age, Siddhartha did not experience the disturbance of **fear or greed**. Despite being brought up amidst the opulence of the palace, Siddhartha did not become obsessed with material wealth or avarice.

This absence of fear and greed initially led Gautama into

a state of confusion. Unlike those around him who pursued their life goals driven by fear or greed, Gautama found himself without such inclinations. This left him feeling restless and uncertain about the purpose of his existence.

While living within the palace, Gautama was scared by Mara to cultivate life goals based on fear, but these attempts failed. Similarly, despite the King's desire for Gautama to become a great ruler driven by greed, this endeavor also proved unsuccessful. Gautama's life purpose became clearer when he first encountered suffering after he reached adulthood.

Gautama engaged in discussions with ascetics to understand why people suffer and how suffering can be eliminated. The conclusion was that suffering could only be eradicated through achieving complete enlightenment. Based on this discussion, Gautama resolved to dedicate his life to becoming an ascetic, with the aim of eliminating suffering and attaining perfect enlightenment.

Fundamentally, Gautama did not experience suffering himself, and his initial ascetic practices were not aimed at eradicating personal suffering. This contrasted with the motivations of other ascetics who engaged in spiritual practices to alleviate their own suffering. Gautama's success in enduring the most extreme forms of suffering was due to his lack of fear and greed, qualities that set him apart from other ascetics who were still influenced by these emotions.

However, after Gautama underwent various forms of suffering through his ascetic practices and reached the brink of death, he realized that he had not found anything substantial. In relinquishing his desire to eliminate suffering and attain enlightenment, Gautama paradoxically achieved perfect enlightenment and became the Buddha.

Fear and greed are among the root causes of human suffering, and the story illustrates that individuals who can conquer fear and master greed will attain enlightenment or perfect consciousness. The nurturing pattern employed by King Suddhodana, characterized by love and compassion, allowed the principles of awareness, pleasure, and vigilance within Siddhartha to operate effectively and optimally, thus preventing him from being dominated by fear and greed.

Gautama's journey is primarily focused on maximizing the function of the awareness principle, while simultaneously attempting to diminish the pleasure principle. He lived based on the principle of awareness, following the teachings of the ascetics to eliminate suffering.

This narrative is particularly interesting because Sigmund Freud predominantly focused on the pleasure principle, while Gautama, approximately 2000 years prior, sought to transcend the pleasure principle and cultivate consciousness, which I refer to as the awareness principle, to achieve enlightenment. Gautama referred to himself as "awakened" once he had achieved enlightenment.

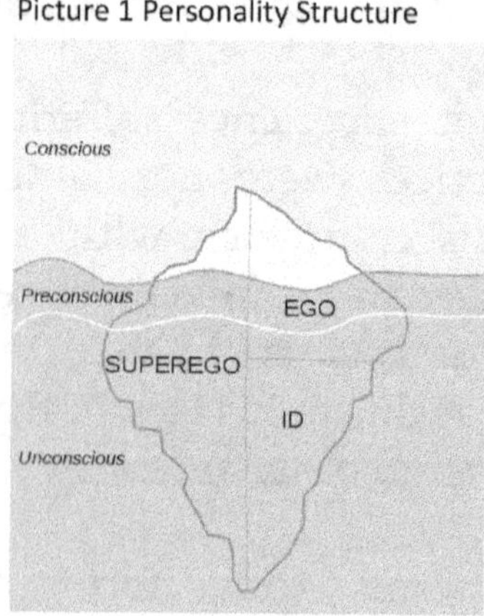

Picture 1 Personality Structure

Source
https://commons.wikimedia.org/wiki/Fil
e:Structural-Iceberg.svg

I do not intend to oversimplify the concept of consciousness in Buddha's teachings. Instead, I aim to provide an alternative perspective that enriches and broadens our understanding of consciousness, particularly in the realm of human psychology. The term **"awareness,"** distinct from the English term **"consciousness,"** encompasses these ideas.

The understanding of the conscious mind is explained by Freud very well, and we will use it in the discussion of awareness and the conscious mind. According to Freud, the conscious mind is part of the structure of personality, which consists of the conscious mind and the subconscious mind. This structure of personality is likened to an iceberg, where the conscious mind is compared to the tip of the iceberg that emerges above the sea surface, while the subconscious mind, which constitutes the majority of the iceberg, is submerged beneath the water.

Freud was not familiar with the term "awareness" and only explained "consciousness." We can assume that they are the same, and perhaps practitioners of meditation or asceticism would explain that perfect awareness is achieved when the entire structure of personality, represented by the iceberg, has been lifted to the surface, so that all actions are fully and perfectly realized without the presence of the subconscious mind.

An example of this training is walking meditation. In walking meditation, the practitioner observes the process of walking step by step, from lifting the foot to placing it down, one stage at a time. This is different from our usual automatic walking, where we walk without explicitly instructing the right or left foot before taking a step.

In essence, walking meditation aims to become fully aware of every movement made while walking, a process that is usually automatic. Some may argue that this form of meditation is pointless, while others may argue the opposite. I will not engage in the debate about this matter[80]. However, from walking meditation, we can draw the conclusion that there is an effort to become aware of a process that previously happened automatically. This effort involves consciously performing actions that were previously automatic, in other words, attempting to bring the entire iceberg to the surface in order to enhance consciousness.

Furthermore, there are various opinions about awareness and consciousness based on individual perceptions. In the teachings of Buddha, the distinction between awareness and consciousness was not made, as Freud introduced the term "consciousness" in the early 20th century. Therefore, the introduction of the awareness principle can clarify the differentiation between awareness and consciousness.

According to the translation of the terms, the awareness principle can be referred to as "awareness", and the conscious mind is consciousness. As a result, within the structure of personality, awareness is no longer part of consciousness; rather, it is a part of the unconscious, specifically residing in the id, which represents basic human instincts. This "awareness" within the unconscious is what I refer to as the awareness principle. Thus, consciousness refers to consciousness itself, while awareness is the awareness principle - two distinct concepts. **Awareness is not consciousness**.

The next question is, what is perfect awareness or perfect enlightenment? If we use the assumption above, the answer is the principle of awareness that is free from fear and functions to the fullest extent, including the principle of pleasure elimination (the higher the level of the awareness principle, the lower the level of the pleasure principle works, and vice versa). According to the story of Buddha, this is something that may be achievable. If this condition can be attained, then vigilance, as a principle, only operates when there is a threat to the awareness principle, while the principle of pleasure no longer exists.

In the teachings of Buddha, the role of meditation is highly emphasized in achieving perfect enlightenment. I would like to provide an additional perspective from the story of Buddha regarding upbringing, where a nurturing **upbringing** filled with compassion enables the awareness principle to function at its maximum potential, thus avoiding disturbances of fear and greed.

The minimal healthy upbringing is to teach vigilance based on **the principle of vigilance,** rather than instilling fear in children or even considering fear as something normal.

The teachings of meditation are equally important, and I will not diminish the significance of the meditation or contemplation process compared to upbringing, especially as a form of therapy to reduce, and if possible, eliminate fear and greed for those trapped within them.

An ideal combination of compassionate nurturing and the practice of meditation or contemplation to enhance the awareness principle is the foundational basis for achieving perfect enlightenment, particularly for those who believe and follow the teachings of Buddha.

The teachings of Buddha are fascinating to explore as they pertain to human psychology and self-discovery. Therefore, allow me to once again embark on a journey using my imagination, delving further into the realm of metaphysics.

The principle of awareness serves the function of self-preservation for living beings, while the principle of pleasure serves the primary purpose of enabling living beings to propagate their offspring. Based on these functions, the principle of awareness takes precedence over the principle of pleasure. In other words, a living organism must ensure or strive for its own self-preservation first before considering the continuation of its lineage, as a function of preserving its species.

It can be said that the awareness principle precedes the pleasure principle; without the awareness principle, the pleasure principle would not exist, while **the awareness principle can still exist without the pleasure principle**.

Just like living beings emerged from inanimate objects, for instance, when the Earth, once inhabited solely by inanimate matter, gradually evolved to create living beings, or in a broader context, when the universe was yet uninhabited by living creatures and slowly evolved on a small planet to give rise to living beings.

If living beings possess the principle of awareness and the principle of pleasure, then inanimate objects that existed prior to living beings would have the principle of awareness without the presence of the principle of pleasure—resulting in an absolute **100%** state of the principle of awareness.

An assumption might go as follows: if every inanimate object has a 100% principle of awareness, signifying an absolute balance that in living beings functions to maintain homeostasis, then the absolute balance in inanimate objects would condition that the structures within them do not change and would remain unchanged indefinitely, only shifting when subjected to external forces or influences.

This naturally differs from living beings who experience structural changes within them over time, necessitating active actions to balance their internal structures, often accomplished through processes like consumption that also rely on the principle of pleasure.

I cannot explain the transformation of inanimate matter into living entities or why the principle of awareness diminishes and evolves into the principle of pleasure, thereby causing inanimate matter to transform into living beings. It's conceivable that specific environments result in particular anomalies in carbon atoms, such that carbon atoms with the ability to form diverse carbon chains become complex chains, becoming too complex to be sustained by the principle of awareness. As a result, the carbon chain system actively forms bonds with other carbon atoms when the chain system is about to break apart. This adaptation ensures the continued existence of the carbon chain system, and we label this complex chain of carbon atoms as a living being.

Yet, how does an overly lengthy chain system suddenly become active in seeking "nourishment"? How does the principle of awareness, which was at 100%, transform into the principle of pleasure, leading the already lengthy carbon chain to develop a system for actively bonding with other carbon atoms to sustain itself? These questions delve into the mysteries of life's creation, and I won't engage in polemics within this context. Therefore, I will return to the assumption of a 100% principle of awareness in inanimate objects.

Based on the assumption that inanimate objects have a 100% principle of awareness. When a human dies, the principle of awareness would increase to 100%, while the principle of pleasure would vanish. The state of a 100% principle of awareness, or "consciousness" in the teachings of Buddhism, was also experienced by Siddhartha Gautama during his meditation as the moon or inanimate matter, where desires based on the principle of pleasure were absent. Thus, Siddhartha Gautama was an individual capable of experiencing **"death"**

while still alive.

The purpose of meditation, as per the interpretation above, is to attain the highest possible state of the principle of awareness, enabling one to "die" while alive. For the contrary holds that if one has died, then (perhaps) they may no longer experience life. There are numerous other benefits of meditation that have been extensively explained, ranging from physical health to mental well-being, heightened wisdom, and many more.

In Indonesia, particularly among the Javanese people, there is a saying: "Eling lan Waspodo." "Eling" translates to "aware" and "waspodo" means "vigilant."[81]. **_Eling lan Waspodo_** can be correlated with the term "awareness" in the teachings of Buddhism. In Javanese culture, two words are used, namely _"eling"_ (aware) and _"waspodo"_ (vigilant), not just "kesadaran" (awareness) alone, as the people of ancient Java understood that it's not just about awareness, but also the need for vigilance.

Even though currently the term awareness widely used to describe this condition, if _"Eling lan Waspodo"_ is equivalent to "awareness" or the effort to achieve perfect enlightenment, then _"eling"_ refers to the principle of awareness which exists in the subconscious mind, not in the conscious mind. And _"waspodo"_ refers, of course, to the principle of vigilance.

The principle of awareness, which is an instinct, operates automatically and will rise to the conscious mind in the form of the principle of vigilance in the presence of a threat. The people of ancient Java have reminded us to preserve these principles of awareness and vigilance to remain rational, not insane. Because in times when the world seems chaotic, it's essential to stay aware and vigilant to remain sane. That's roughly the advice from Ronggowarsito[82].

Spiritual practitioners who strive for enlightenment or full awareness, according to this theory, seek to enhance the principle of awareness towards 100%, resembling inanimate objects through practices such as meditation, solitude, or deep contemplation.

Some paths attempt to increase awareness by deliberately reducing comfort, but based on the insights from this theory, achieving enlightenment requires addressing disturbances first, particularly **fear and greed**, rather than intentionally diminishing comfort. Indulging in delicious food, enjoying life, and similar experiences are pleasurable ways to satisfy the principle of pleasure, yet the attachment to these can be hazardous, especially greed rather than the mere **fulfillment of pleasure**. The principle of pleasure diminishes naturally once it is fulfilled due to the presence of the principles of awareness and vigilance, **"Eling lan Waspodo."**

To achieve a healthy balance between the principles of awareness and pleasure, or for those aspiring to be spiritual practitioners aiming to elevate awareness to 100%, it is essential to be free from the disturbance of fear, much like Prince Siddhartha Gautama. His **upbringing** by King Suddhodana, where he was shielded from suffering and nurtured with love, allowed him to grow up without fear.

For individuals who wish to embark on a spiritual path but are entangled in the disturbances of fear and greed, addressing these disturbances is crucial. This can be achieved through various therapies, whether by seeking professional help or through spiritual practices such as tapa (austerity), meditation, or other spiritual methods, with the right understanding and purpose. Merely attempting to suppress the principle or urge of pleasure with strict discipline will not be successful.

For instance, if one is still dominated by fear and greed, engaging in austerity, meditation, or spiritual practices can help alleviate these feelings. However, one should not expect these practices to elevate the principle of awareness to 100% or attain perfect enlightenment until fear and greed have been eliminated.

The principle of awareness can be honed through austerity, meditation, or mindfulness to prevent falling into deeper states of fear and greed. It can only be honed as a form of guardianship or an initial function of the principle of awareness, serving as a overseer with limits for the buried fears and desires within oneself.

If an individual is content with their condition, along with the fear or greed within their subconscious, and can maintain a comfortable and harmonious life, they are free to live with gratitude. However, if an individual desires to elevate their principle of awareness to 100%, they need to reduce fear and greed. Only when these are eradicated 100%, can they be equated with having the principle of awareness, similar to **young Prince Siddhartha, who had not yet attained perfect enlightenment**. Afterward, the individual can once again embark on the journey to achieve perfect enlightenment, the 100% principle of awareness. It's a truly long path to achieve perfect enlightenment, and it is commendable if there are individuals striving for it.

Nevertheless, based on the basic functioning of human instincts, the concept of 100% awareness contradicts the innate human drive to evolve based on pleasure principles. Additionally, many opinions argue that suffering stems from desires driven by the libido, which operates according to pleasure principles.

However, the root of the issue lies not in the realm of desires, but rather in disruptions to the vigilance principle in facing threats; situations where vigilance should prevail are replaced by fear or anger. Hence, the ideal human life would involve operating in accordance with their basic instincts while also maintaining the functioning of the vigilance principle to prevent disturbances, ensuring that they do not get oppressed too frequently or experience trauma.

CHAPTER 11
CIVILIZATIONAL EVOLUTION

Let us imagine that an absolutely unbiased observer on another planet, perhaps on Mars, is examining human behaviour on earth, with the aid of a telescope whose magnification is too small to enable him to discern individuals and follow their separate behaviour, but large enough for him to observe occurrences such as migration of peoples, wars and similar great historical events. He would never gain the impression that human behaviour was dictated by intelligence, still less by responsible morality[83].
Konrad Lorenz

Human modern civilization when writing was introduced as the beginning of recorded history can generally be divided into three stages of civilization evolution. The first evolution is the kingdom system, where the king becomes the leader of the civilization. This evolution occurred when societies began to settle in a particular area and were led by a leader of the community.

This civilization of kingdoms developed over a long period, starting from the time of ancient Egypt and generally ending with the fall of the Roman Empire. Although in other parts of the world, the kingdom system still existed. After the decline of the kingdom system, the next evolution of civilization occurred, which was the religious system. In this stage, religion played the most significant role in a civilization, shifting the focus from the king or kingdom. Once the religious system no longer dominated human civilization, the next evolution emerged, bringing forth the economic system as its dominant force.

The Kingdom System

Let's begin with the first evolution of human civilization in recorded history, which is the kingdom system. I call it an evolution of civilization because the process took a long time, spanning hundreds or even thousands of years, although not as long as the evolution in living organisms that can take millions of years. I use the term "kingdom system" rather than just "kingdom" because I am more focused on the system itself rather than the kingdom as a whole.

During the early stages of recorded history, when human civilization was able to establish cities and governance systems, kingdoms began to emerge, usually led by a king or queen. The ruler of the kingdom became the central authority, wielding immense power over their governance. In some kingdoms around the world, the king was even regarded as a deity or a divine being.

The substantial power held by the king over their subjects meant that the fate of the people was deeply intertwined with the ruler's decisions. This encompassed everything from basic necessities like food and shelter to matters of life and death. The magnitude of the king's authority created a sense of dependence among the people, leading to a natural fear of the king, as their lives hinged on the ruler's wisdom.

People would strive to fulfill the desires or commands of the king in order to secure their safety, well-being, and prosperity. Even a benevolent king would inspire fear due to the extent of the people's reliance on them. This dependence could be even more pronounced under a tyrannical ruler, one who used their military might to suppress and control the population. In such cases, fear among the people would be intensified.

Every ruler in power desired loyalty from their subjects and aimed to prevent any form of rebellion. During the era of kingdoms, people would remain loyal to their king either out of reverence for their wisdom or out of fear. For a king in this era, being wise was not an easy task, as they faced the temptation of using their unparalleled power to act as they pleased. The easiest option for a king to gain obedience from the people and to steer the wheels of governance was often to invoke fear, utilizing the strength of their military forces. This marked the creation of a system that could induce **mass fear**, an ability harnessed by a mere mortal.

Before the establishment of the kingdom system, humans were primarily fearful of natural disasters. However, after the emergence of the kingdom system, the populace also became fearful of their kings. Even the wisest of kings would still be feared by their subjects due to their tremendous power.

Ordinary people, commonly referred to as the commoners or the masses, generally harbored fear towards the kingdom's military, which represented the king. They aspired to serve the kingdom or enter the palace environment. For the commoners, this could be achieved by pursuing careers as soldiers, traders, or experts in fields that the kingdom required.

In this kingdom system, the wealthiest individuals were typically the kings themselves. No commoner's wealth exceeded that of the king, not even a skilled trader within the kingdom. This concentration of wealth within the king's hands elevated the king to a central position, becoming the aspiration of individuals such as the king's siblings, nobles, or landowners who were wealthy enough to raise armies.

Many tales of kingdoms revolve around rebellions, coups, and betrayals aimed at seizing the throne. For the king's siblings and nobles, they held both fear and ambition towards the king. For the commoners, their fear of the ruler existed, but they lacked the courage to aspire for wealth, let alone power.

The primary ambition for commoners was to serve the kingdom, regardless of who the king was. However, if the king was particularly fearsome, even surviving and living decently became a struggle for the commoners.

The kingdom system, which caused widespread fear of rulers among the people, endured for a considerable time, spanning thousands of years before the Common Era. This system persisted into the early Common Era and was still prevalent in some regions, particularly in Asia and Africa, until the Middle Ages. Over time, its power diminished with the development of various governance systems.

The transformation from the kingdom system started around the early Common Era, coinciding with the emergence of various belief systems and faiths that birthed religions. This process was initially instigated by religious and spiritual advisers—individuals skilled in conducting various rituals within the palace and who often doubled as spiritual counselors to the king.

Over time, these spiritual and religious experts gained influence through popular support driven by religious zealotry. High levels of zealotry wielded considerable power, which led kings to tread cautiously when dealing with such religious fervor. The spread of militant religions forced kings into compromises, as these fervent adherents were difficult to control or suppress, even through military force. This second evolution can generally be traced back to the spread of Christianity and its transition from a localized movement to a global belief system.

Religious Evolution

Beginning with the spread of Christianity, Jesus's followers disseminated the faith throughout the region surrounding Israel, eventually reaching the heart of the Roman

Empire in Rome. Despite being pursued by Roman forces, these followers remained steadfast in spreading the Christian faith across various regions. The apostle Paul played a pioneering role in this spread.

In the early Common Era, the Roman Empire's power began to wane due to leadership weaknesses, resulting in reduced prosperity for the populace. It was during this time that Christianity offered a promise of an otherworldly paradise, in contrast to the mundane world, which was warmly embraced by a frustrated populace. They abandoned their old gods, whom they deemed inadequate in providing solutions[84].

The descendants of the Greek people are among those who predominantly embraced Christianity, owing to their inclination towards open-mindedness due to the advancement of Greek philosophy. This, combined with their sense of despair caused by the decline of the Roman Empire, led them to welcome the new teaching of a single God with open arms, replacing their multitude of deities.

As the number of Christian followers within the Roman Empire grew, and with the increasing intensity of Germanic attacks, Emperor Constantine legalized Christianity in Rome. Subsequent emperors then declared Catholic Christianity as the official religion of the Roman Empire, due to the growing Christian population, led by a Pope. Following these developments, the Western Roman Empire eventually collapsed, unable to withstand the onslaught of Germanic forces.

In its subsequent development, the Catholic Church adopted the governance system of the Roman Empire. This included a Pope with a position akin to an Emperor, alongside Bishops who held leadership roles in regions or provinces, and Chief Priests as leaders of local churches. This governance system carried forward the structure of the Roman Empire and has persisted to the present day[85].

Subsequently, the power of the Catholic Church grew, especially in Europe, and at a certain point, it even surpassed the authority of local rulers or kings. The immense power of the

Pope resulted from a shift in spiritual authority. In the previous era of kingdoms, the king was considered a representative of God or a deity, even seen as an embodiment of the divine. However, within the religious system, rulers lost this position, which was then taken over by religious leaders acting as representatives of God.

In the context of the Catholic Church, especially during the Middle Ages in Europe, the Pope assumed the role of God's representative, and local kings were no longer the spiritual leaders in their respective regions. As society transitioned into this era, where religious figures held more power than kings, a form of fear of God emerged, mediated by these religious authorities.

This fear was predominantly cultivated through the concept of sin and the impending punishment awaiting sinners. The punishments for sins, as dictated by religious leaders, included severe consequences, even up to loss of life. During the Middle Ages, a significant number of women were executed, accused of sin and often labeled as witches[86].

This period saw a significant intertwining of religious authority and political power, and fear of divine retribution played a crucial role in maintaining control over the populace. Fear of God or gods during the era of kingdoms still existed, but the people were more focused on the figure of the king who represented God or gods, or even became a manifestation of the gods themselves. However, when religion gained a stronger position than the government led by the king, the people became more fearful of God, especially afraid of being punished for sins, and this was exploited by the "representatives" of God to control the society.

During the time of kingdoms, when there was a king who represented a deity, in the era of religion, people directly worshipped God, not the religious leaders as representatives of God. Nevertheless, religious leaders still had the ability to use the name of God as a tool to control the society. One well-known form of abuse was the selling of letters of confession of sins in the Catholic Church during the Middle Ages[87].

During this era, religion became the center of human civilization, where people's primary goal was to serve God. Leaders, rulers, or kings followed as figures after God. This is different from the era of kingdoms where people's main goal was to serve the king.

The focus on the "will" of God created a distinct form of fanaticism within society, often exploited by religious leaders for their personal gain. Furthermore, this fanaticism towards God could mobilize masses to defend their God or take up arms to spread His teachings.

While in medieval Europe under the influence of Catholic religious leaders, in the Middle East, Islam was established with its founder, Prophet Muhammad, forming a caliphate to spread Islam across various regions in the Middle East and North Africa. These two major forces eventually clashed, leading to the famous Crusades[88].

The high fear of God, especially concerning His prohibitions that could result in sin if violated, could lead to punishment not only by religious leaders but also by the community with a high level of fanaticism in carrying out God's will as interpreted by religious leaders and followed by the believers of that religion. For those who refuse to obey the orders or the will of God, they could be labeled as sinners.

Both of these aspects, the fear of God and the fanatical attitude towards one's religion, are characteristic of societies during the medieval period that were dominated by religious organizations which also held power over the governance system, such as the Catholic Church in Europe and Islam in the Middle East.

In Indonesia itself, during the medieval period, the country still followed a system of Kingdom governance with numerous kingdoms existing in the region. Indonesia has never been ruled by a single religion, even though the majority of the population in Indonesia currently adheres to Islam.

By the end of the Majapahit kingdom era, Islam finally

arrived in Indonesia. While Islam had reached Sumatra long before, the systematic spread of Islamic teachings took place during the latter part of the Majapahit era, facilitated by the Champa kingdom in Vietnam[89]. However, the teachings that entered Indonesia were adapted to the Indonesian culture, so that the Indonesian culture was not abandoned, although there is still a group of people who desire a purer form of Islam like in the Middle East.

This practice continues to this day, even though local cultures are gradually fading, and our society tends to adopt more Arab or Western influences. Then, the Portuguese arrived in Indonesia, followed by the Dutch, who became the new rulers, marking the entry of human civilization into the era of European colonialism across the world, which paved the way for the next evolution of human civilization.

The fundamental difference between the fear of a king in a monarchy system and the fear of God in a religious system lies in the fact that fear of a king is fear of something concrete – the physical presence of a king, whereas fear of God is fear of something abstract because the true nature of God cannot be grasped by the human senses.

The abstract fear of God is represented by religious leaders within the religious system, so that people are actually not afraid of the religious leaders themselves, but rather afraid of God's punishment, which is implemented by the religious leaders. This is different from the fear of a king or the fear of gods that manifest in the form of a king, where people fear a physical king.

As time went on, society became increasingly critical of religious leaders who used the name of God to carry out arbitrary actions for their own benefit. People began to doubt whether religious leaders truly represented the voice of God or their own voice, especially in matters related to knowledge.

There emerged conflicts between scientific knowledge and religious knowledge, especially within the Catholic Church in Europe. This reached its peak with the trial of Galileo Galilei by the Catholic Church due to his conflicting views with the Church's belief that the Earth was the center of the solar system versus Galileo's assertion that the Sun was the center[90].

This conflict marked the weakening influence of the Catholic Church in Europe over human civilization and signaled the onset of the next evolution of civilization, characterized by the rise of knowledge, starting with the Renaissance era and culminating in the Industrial Revolution, which heralded the beginning of the evolution of the current human civilization, where economic systems dominate.

Economic System

The resurgence of European culture, known as the Renaissance, in the 14th century marked the beginning of critical thinking about the prevailing system of the time, namely the religious system. Initiated by the critical thinking of great artists, the development of scientific thought began in Europe, with a growing number of critical thinkers signaling the onset of the industrial revolution era.

The rapid development of scientific knowledge continued until the early 20th century, culminating in the contributions of great scientists like Albert Einstein, a Jewish figure who propelled human civilization into the modern era. As human civilization entered the era of the industrial revolution, industries rapidly flourished in various European countries, with each nation competing to control various commodities used as industrial raw materials.

This situation prompted European nations to search for raw materials and commodities in their original source countries, leading to massive maritime expeditions by European nations around the world and marking the era of colonialism. This colonialism involved European powers colonizing the indigenous populations of various regions, including the Dutch and Portuguese colonization in Indonesia.

During the industrial revolution era, the knowledge

developed was used to advance industrialization, leading to increased production of goods for sale. In order to maintain production, the produced goods had to be purchased, necessitating a functioning industrial economic system. However, due to the rapid growth of industries, overproduction occurred as the demand and income of the population did not align with the quantity of goods produced. This situation contributed to the significant economic crisis of the 1930s[91].

The economic system underwent further reforms, but at that time, it had not fully succeeded in completely dominating human civilization. Efforts were made to ensure that the overall money circulating in society was sufficient to purchase the produced goods, thereby preventing shortages of money for buying goods. This goal was eventually achieved with the introduction of paper currency, replacing precious metal coins which were limited in quantity based on the amount of precious metal owned by a government[92].

Furthermore, experts in sales and marketing, drawing from Sigmund Freud's theory of libido, successfully transformed the world's economic system by enticing consumers to spend their money to experience pleasure, comfort, and luxury. This approach triggered the consumer's pleasure principle, compelling individuals to buy goods not necessarily out of need but because they desired them. This phenomenon has evolved into what we now refer to as consumerism, where people develop a habitual pattern of consumption driven by desires rather than actual needs[93],[94].

After the industrial revolution, the economic system practically took over human civilization, replacing the religious system. However, the existing economic system was not yet stable, and a battle between two economic systems emerged: communism versus capitalism. This intense rivalry between the two economic systems had profound impacts, even influencing forms of governance. This demonstrates the close relationship between a government's economic system and its governing structure.

As time progressed, capitalism emerged as the clear winner in this economic clash and became the dominant system used by nearly all countries around the world, including those that might not officially identify as capitalist but still operate under capitalist economic principles due to the global trade regulations influenced by capitalism.

With the invention of television and the widespread dissemination of information, economic promotion evolved into a massively influential form through television advertisements. However, this wasn't just about advertising products; it was about disseminating an entire civilization through television. The human civilization controlled by the capitalist economic system was spread through this medium.

Society became continually bombarded by forms of information capable of controlling the masses through subconscious triggers, such as the unconscious libido. This created desires and habits that were collectively accepted and evolved into the capitalist civilization. We are often unaware of this process, feeling that we can control our desires and that our wants are reasonable and not driven by greed.

Nevertheless, it is clear that our society has fallen into a culture of consumerism. What we don't know is where this originated. We are not aware that the capitalist economic civilization has taken over human civilization. Capitalism spreads through the subconscious mind, triggering desires like **greed**. And it's not just libido; other systems have been developed as well, including the one proven effective since the time of kingdoms: **fear**.

A strong economic system must be supported by an education system and a workforce that aligns with that economic system, in this case, the capitalist system. The first condition is to maintain mass fear, similar to what was done in religious and monarchy systems. This condition is already fulfilled as contemporary human civilization accepts fear as a part of daily life. This fear is not used to easily manipulate society, but rather it's developed in the form of anxiety and frustration. Humans fear poverty and desire quick wealth or greed, and this is driven by various propaganda in media such as advertisements, films, soap operas, and news.

The second condition is the existence of a supporting system that allows these fears, anxieties, and greed to flourish. This is facilitated through the education system and the prevailing mindset in the workforce. The educational system that emphasizes competition, individualism, and ranking is the foundation for shaping generations that are highly driven to possess everything or become greedy. This mindset is further developed in the workforce where an atmosphere of competition prevails, where individuals strive to succeed.

Although this lifestyle might seem acceptable and modern, it's important to delve into the education system. The Indonesian government has begun to recognize the need to break free from an education system that produces a capitalist-oriented generation. There is a realization that something has been wrong with our education system.

Education System in Indonesia

One major concern in Indonesia is the lack of true experts in their fields. This is evident in the scarcity of university graduates in Indonesia who work according to their specific expertise. Most graduates in Indonesia, upon graduating, aspire to become civil servants to secure a stable income and retirement benefits. This desire extends not only to the graduates but also to their parents who wish their children to become civil servants, and even hope for their children to marry someone working in the government.

Only a small number of graduates are interested in further developing their expertise. Those pursuing higher degrees like Master's or PhDs often prioritize advancing their career before focusing on their knowledge expansion. While Indonesia has a considerable number of intelligent individuals, few are willing to become experts within the country. Many choose to study abroad due to the weakness of Indonesia's education system, causing the loss of local talents in various fields.

Another crucial weakness is the lack of critical thinking rooted in ethics and social morals. While many Indonesians are capable of criticism, it's often driven by personal or group gains, such as politicians and television commentators. The current critical thinking in Indonesia is a result of competitive products within the education system. Intelligent individuals in Indonesia are skilled at critiquing their competitors, but lack the capability to critically evaluate problems objectively. This stems from the fact that they were never taught to do so from an early age. The behavior cultivated in basic education is centered on competition to become a champion, including evaluating competitors' weaknesses. This behavior is prominently seen during elections.

Basic education, or elementary school, is an advanced form of education following parental upbringing. Even though it's referred to as "basic," it's actually advanced education because true foundational education occurs at home. Our upbringing assumes fear is a basic human emotion, leading parents to believe that instilling fear in their children is normal. It's not uncommon to hear that a child should fear their **father** to ensure obedience. This condition means that every child entering elementary school is already equipped with fear.

As if in "harmony", the world of education explores this fear as part of the education system that supports capitalism. First, through homework, where children are given tasks to be completed at home and will be punished by their teachers if they don't do their homework, which creates a fear in children not to neglect their homework. In Indonesia itself, the benefits of homework are already being examined, and even in Purwakarta, homework has been prohibited from being given to students[95].

Then the next fear is the fear of getting poor grades, which makes children afraid of being scolded by their parents and teachers, especially when facing exams, particularly the National Examinations. In Indonesia, the National Examinations have been eliminated for Elementary Schools. Lastly, a form of education that supports capitalism is competition, which is trained from elementary school through ranking systems. Fortunately, in some schools, the ranking system has already been eliminated[96].

Actually, competition is a form of psychological development that is important for humans to adapt to their environment. However, schools cannot guarantee **psychologically healthy competition** for their students, resulting in competition only generating psychological disturbances for both winners and losers. For those who win, it leads to greed, while those who lose feel like losers and lose self-confidence.

Imagine that these feelings have to be experienced by elementary school children to sharpen their greed and fears. The level of competition among students in the Indonesian education system has started to be reduced, and an understanding is being developed to nurture the uniqueness and strengths of each student, with the hope that the nation will have the necessary professional workforce.

Capitalist Competition

Excessive competition only produces a generation dominated by fear and greed, lacking critical thinking skills to address real issues but having strong criticism towards competitors. This is most evident in the political competition during elections in Indonesia, where news is more focused on attacking political opponents rather than explaining the programs that will solve the existing problems. This stems from the fact that from an early age, our politicians are accustomed to unhealthy competition, directing their critical thinking towards attacking opponents rather than finding solutions.

This unhealthy competitive education forms the foundation for creating skilled workers for the capitalist economy. These are workers who are willing to work hard to be the best, eliminating unproductive workers. This leads to highly productive workers who benefit companies, with reduced critical thinking about the existing system. As a result, these workers won't ask too many questions, will remain loyal, and will accept incomes that don't match the effort they put into the company – a form of **exploitation** that often occurs in irresponsible private companies.

Meanwhile, for workers engaged in competitive capitalism, those who do not emerge triumphant are relegated to lives of hardship, poverty, and fear. Conversely, even victorious competitors find themselves ensnared in a conundrum of distress, avarice, fear, and wealth, although the latter often comes at the cost of their mental well-being, leading to job burnout or **work-related stress**.

However, this does not imply that there are no workers who genuinely thrive and derive satisfaction from their endeavors. Certainly, there are those who manage to savor the fruits of their labor and extricate themselves from the system to relish life and their occupations. This is attainable for workers who possess the requisite critical acumen to navigate the capitalist milieu without becoming entrapped within it.

The purpose of competition within the capitalist economic framework is to foster a workforce that is perpetually insatiable, driven by greed, and ceaselessly strives for more. Such an environment cultivates productive employees that serve to bolster company profits. Yet, companies expend meager sums in compensating these employees, simultaneously demanding greater exertion for enhanced remuneration. This results in enterprises reaping substantial gains from the strenuous efforts of their staff, leaving minimal proportions of the generated profits for the diligent workers themselves.

Conversely, unproductive workers are left with

diminished self-esteem, often scrambling for any available employment to secure income. Successful employees, on the other hand, are perennially discontented, ceaselessly enticed by the promise of unending success, rendering them increasingly covetous. This dynamic pushes them to embrace whatever means necessary, including the morally reprehensible act of corruption, in their relentless pursuit of prosperity and affluence. Simultaneously, workers who lose out in the competitive race are not exempt from the snares of avarice, as the onslaught of media messages instigates their consumerist tendencies.

Amidst the contrast between thriving workers and those scraping by, both categories share an inherent avariciousness. Successful workers are overtaken by intensified greed, with their fears and anxieties nearly completely transformed into a dependency on avarice. Meanwhile, workers who merely subsist contend with greater apprehensions and worries than their tendencies for greed, manifesting primarily as fears of impoverishment, an uncertain future, and various other uncertainties.

Naturally, since greed fundamentally stems from a dependency on frustration and fear, the apprehensions experienced by workers leading modest lives are no greater in magnitude than those encountered by productive and successful workers. Both categories share a commonality in their fears, worries, and frustrations. Within the capitalist system, there are no winners among workers; the beneficiaries are those who **wield capital**, not the labor force.

The system will attempt to make successful workers have lower critical acumen so that they don't become owners of capital and remain productive workers. This is achieved by enticing their libido to become consumeristic. However, if they are clever enough, these workers may also become capitalists and continue the capitalist system by exploiting workers who will work for them.

Of course, the number of workers who successfully

become capitalists is very small, and they are the ones at the top of the capitalist economic pyramid. Large capitalists always prevail over small ones within the capitalist economic system. Therefore, workers must work hard to amass significant capital before they can compete with large capitalists.

It's extremely difficult for small capitalists to compete with larger ones, unless they manage to break out of the system by creating their own, or possess specific skills they can leverage to compete with the big capitalists. However, the number of workers in these situations is negligible and not significant enough to change the overpowering capitalist system.

Meanwhile, the majority of workers aspire to become bosses of large companies or to own their own businesses, regardless of whether they have strong abilities or just average ones. These aspirations are propagated by capitalist propaganda, driving everyone to desire success through capitalist competition.

Within the framework of capitalist competition, there are only two desired psychological states for workers according to big capital: greed or fear, the fear of poverty, unemployment, or lack of money. Fear and greed become everyday psychological conditions experienced by the population and workers in general, serving as tools for the capitalist economic system to control human civilization.

A notable distinction between the capitalist economic system and religious or monarchical systems is that while the latter use fear to control civilization, capitalism employs greed and fear to achieve the same goal. In monarchical or religious eras, only the king, nobles, or those close to religious leaders might be consumed by greed, while the common people were more governed by fear, hoping for prosperity dependent on their rulers. However, in the capitalist system, even **ordinary people can become greedy**.

The rapid advancement of industries, leading to a sharp increase in production and easy accessibility of goods, along with advancements in marketing strategies that appeal to the satisfaction of libido-driven desires, has driven society towards greed. This phenomenon has become a cultural norm, softened by the term **"consumerism,"** which has infected every layer of society, whether rich or poor.

On the other hand, the liberal competition in the effort of people striving to achieve wealth has created a distinct fear – the fear of losing in competition and becoming poor, devoid of a future, a loser, and other derogatory terms coined by capitalist society to magnify fear. The hope is that this fear will serve as motivation for the "losers" to revert to greed or even complete despair, so as not to disrupt the pursuits of their competitors.

The state of the capitalist economy demonstrates the presence of equal opportunities in the economic field, allowing even the common people to dream of becoming wealthy. While this aspiration remains difficult to achieve, this dream has caused the common folk to also be captivated by greed, previously a characteristic mainly attributed to the ruling class. Thus, a **redistribution of greed** has occurred in this capitalist economic era.

Meanwhile, the redistribution of wealth remains but a dream. The ruling class continues to be the wealthiest, while the masses remain impoverished, a situation that has persisted from the monarchical era to the present day. This perpetuates the widening gap between the rich and the poor.

Capitalist economics introduces unrestricted competition, where everyone, whether rich or poor, can compete to become wealthier economically. Economists have formulated various economic laws to ensure global economies continue to run steadily and increase their total wealth. Despite economic fluctuations, the overarching goal is for wealth to consistently grow.

Humans, as subjects of capitalist economics, are continually pushed to work hard and compete to enhance their individual wealth, whether for basic needs or non-essential desires. Economists claim to have established rules and economic laws that promote healthy competition based on justice, akin to "fair play" in sports. However, the reality of economic competition is far from fair play; it's highly competitive and often lacks fairness.

In contrast to the economic realm, the sports world emphasizes creating rules as fair as possible, allowing losers to accept them while achieving victories through just means, fostering **pride** rather than greed. Athletes are also expected to maintain strong psychological or mental states during competition, staying focused without being driven by the desire to win, and not succumbing to self-doubt or fear when facing opponents.

This greatly contrasts with the realm of capitalist economic competition, where individuals strive to harness their every bit of greed, as long as it doesn't violate criminal or civil laws, to defeat their opponents. Victims of this competition, initially driven by greed, are at risk of experiencing other psychological disturbances such as stress, reduced clarity of thought, and even progressing to depression, which can lead to more severe psychological disorders.

Competition within capitalist economics, fueled by greed and fear, clearly fails to deliver economic justice to human civilization. The widening wealth gap and increasing poverty highlight that the wealthy are becoming greedier, while the poor are becoming more fearful.

Fundamentally, competition is essential for human development, but it should be limited to promoting aggression or for enjoyment and pride, as seen in the world of sports. When competition yields fear and greed, it has evolved into an unhealthy state for human civilization. Regrettably, we have accepted this unhealthy competition and turned greed into a culture we call **consumerism.**

Capitalist economy operates through a system of competition among individuals, followed by competition among companies, and ultimately competition among nations. This competition, which breeds greed and fear, has not succeeded in bringing about peace, as wars persist and terrorism has emerged, both of which fundamentally represent economic battles over resources like oil and minerals.

When humans compete with each other over natural resources, the environment becomes excessively exploited, leading to its degradation, including **global warming**. People are so engrossed in competing against each other that they engage in conflicts, forgetting the natural environment or the planet Earth they inhabit.

While each individual, group, company, or nation is busy competing and prioritizing their own interests, humanity as a whole forgets to consider the well-being of the planet Earth, which is crucial for sustaining human civilization.

While intellectuals are busy developing various fields of knowledge, technologies, economic and political systems to support the dominant economic structure, only volunteers or activists tend to think about the safety of the environment on this planet. However, these volunteers or activists cannot compete with the progress in various fields of knowledge that support the industrial economic system.

Capitalist economy essentially evolved from cultures in regions with harsh environments, where people had to confront the challenges of nature and compete against each other to fulfill basic needs for self-preservation. This is exemplified in regions like the Middle East, where since ancient times, people have been competing for control over riverside areas, or in Europe, where they had to combat severe winters.

Conversely, there are regions where the environment is more hospitable, and competition among humans isn't as necessary because nature provides all that's needed for basic sustenance. Tropical areas in Southeast Asia, Latin America, or South Asia serve as examples.

There are also harsh regions where only a few people can survive due to their intellectual abilities driven by a strong desire for self-preservation. They manage to create the necessary technologies to thrive in such challenging environments, as seen in Northern Europe.

Currently, human civilization possesses advanced technologies, rendering harsh environments less of a threat. However, the competitive culture brought by European nations has transformed into capitalist economy, spreading worldwide, including in areas that inherently have friendly, comfortable, and beautiful natural environments, such as Indonesia.

Nevertheless, due to the influence of capitalist economy, Indonesian society now tends to confront nature by deforesting for industry, instead of utilizing the local flora for daily life. One of the consequences of the proliferation of capitalist economic system is competition, which poses a challenge to Indonesian when compared to others more accustomed to competitive environments.

Our difficulty in competing stems from the fact that our ancestors were not accustomed to competing against each other; they were more accustomed to **communal cooperation "gotong royong"**. The Indonesian government is now responding fairly well to the challenges posed by capitalist economic competition with other nations by avoiding becoming ensnared in the capitalist economic system and by developing a people-oriented economic system based on familial and cooperative principles, rather than ruthless competition, even though this remains primarily a political slogan[97].

Dystopia vs Utopia

The capitalist economic system not only brings about competition among humans, but also between humans and nature. In order to manifest human greed in the form of productivity and accumulating possessions, nature becomes the victim. Capitalist economics can be likened to **digging its own grave**; we are harming the environment, which is essentially our home.

We are damaging the environment in the name of economy, in the name of greed, in the name of economic competition, and in the pursuit of wealth. When the environment is damaged, human civilization will die. We call this dystopia, a bleak future for the planet where only the wealthy manage to survive the environmental devastation. However, in this grim future, the distinction between the rich and the poor disappears, as the poor vanish.

The poor will not be able to compete with the rich anymore, and their competition will not be for wealth driven by greed, but for survival due to the deteriorated environment, driven by the fear of extinction. Meanwhile, the remnants of human civilization, the wealthy, will try to sustain themselves with technology they have developed in response to the harsh environment.

The future of capitalist economics is **the degradation of the environment**. The next evolution of human civilization from the capitalist economic system will be an environmental degradation system. This new era will be ruled by fear, the fear of extinction due to the ruined environment that renders the Earth uninhabitable. Once again, human civilization will unite to confront the environment that has turned into a threat to humanity.

If there's dystopia, there's also utopia – an ideal future when the capitalist economic system is abandoned, and human civilization enters the next stage of evolution. This evolution begins with **liberating humanity from fear and anger**, which are the main enemies of humans. It involves liberating humanity from fear, which is used as a tool to control society, whether consciously or unconsciously, and from anger and frustration, which are the sources of greed and various psychological disturbances.

It all starts with parenting, when a mother no longer considers fear as something natural, when a mother no longer considers fear as an inherent basic emotion, when a mother no longer deliberately uses anger to instill fear in her baby, when a mother no longer allows her baby to feel fear, and when a mother teaches her child to be **vigilant** instead of resorting to fear and anger in raising them.

This will result in future generations with healthy and reasonable critical thinking abilities, generations that can criticize the existing system, generations that are free from fear and greed, and generations that can harness their critical and creative faculties to seek solutions and establish a civilization system that is healthier for both physical and mental well-being, all while harmonizing with the natural world.

Fear and anger will be considered as forms of psychological disturbances, just like any other psychological disorders, and are recognized as dangerous. So, when someone experiences fear and anger, they will immediately be assisted in overcoming these emotions.

Ultimately, an evolution of human civilization will be created that is free from fear and greed. This will open the gateway for humanity's next adventures in evolution, eventually leading to physical evolution.

Utopia,
Welcome to a civilization without fear and greed.

THE END

=====================================

[1] https://id.wikipedia.org/wiki/Astronomi_Mesir

[2] https://id.wikipedia.org/wiki/Kalender_Maya

[3] https://id.wikipedia.org/wiki/Stonehenge#cite_note-9

[4]   https://tekno.tempo.co/read/news/2017/05/09/095873602/stephen-hawking-manusia-hanya-punya-waktu-
  100-tahun

[5] https://en.wikipedia.org/wiki/Death_drive[6].
  Laplanche, Jean; Pontalis, Jean-Bertrand (1973). "Instinct (or Drive) (pp. 214-7)". The Language of Psychoanalysis. London: Karnac Books. ISBN 978-0-946-43949-2. ISBN 0-94643949-4

[6] https://en.wikipedia.org/wiki/Death_drive "Origin of the theory: Beyond the Pleasure Principle"

[7]   http://news.detik.com/berita/2833677/mensos-khofifah-usul-hukuman-putus-syaraf-libido-bagi-pelaku-
  kejahatan-seksual

[8] https://en.wikipedia.org/wiki/Mortido#cite_note-3

[9] Sarwono, W. Sarlito., "Berkenalan dengan aliran-aliran dan tokoh-tokoh psikologi". Bulan
  Bintang, 2002, hlm. 155-156.

[10] Ibid., hlm.157.

[11] Ibid

[12] Ibid., hlm.164.

[13] Ibid., hlm. 158.

[14] Ibid., hlm. 159.

[15] Lorenz, Konrad., "On Aggresion", Routledge, 2002, hlm. 101.

[16] https://en.wikipedia.org/wiki/Fight-or-flight_response#cite_note-2[1].
  Cannon, Walter (1932). Wisdom of the Body. United States: W.W. Norton & Company. ISBN 0393002055

[17] Sarwono, W. Sarlito., "Psikologi Sosial". Balai Pustaka, 2002., hlm. 305.

[18] Ibid., hlm. 306.

[19] Ibid., hlm. 307-308.

[20] Ibid., hlm. 298.

[21] http://kengracun.blogspot.co.id/2011/03/psikologi-sosial.html[4]
https://www.ncjrs.gov/App/Publications/abstract.aspx?ID=55082
Moyer, KE., "Kinds of aggression and their physiological basis (Abstrac)". Journal : Communications in Behavioral Biology 2A:65-87

[22] Ibid

[23] https://en.wikipedia.org/wiki/Homeostasis

[24] https://id.wikipedia.org/wiki/Fisiologi_manusia "Konsep Homeostasis".

[25] https://id.wikipedia.org/wiki/Hipotalamus

[26] Pinel, P.J. John., "Biopsikologi". Pustaka Pelajar, 2009, hlm. 68.

[27] https://en.wikipedia.org/wiki/Autonomic_nervous_system

[28] https://en.wikipedia.org/wiki/Epinephrine

[29] https://www.cnnindonesia.com/gaya-hidup/20150306114628-255-37181/dehidrasi-tekanan-panas-dan-kematian/

[30] Pinel, P.J. John., "Biopsikologi". Pustaka Pelajar, 2009, hlm. 252-256.

[31] http://www.materisma.com/2014/06/sistem-saraf-pada-manusia.html

[32] Pinel, P.J. John., "Biopsikologi". Pustaka Pelajar, 2009, hlm. 257-260.

[33] Ibid., hlm.68.

[34] https://en.wikipedia.org/wiki/Epinephrine

[35] https://id.wikipedia.org/wiki/Persepsi

[36] https://www.nsf.gov/mobile/discoveries/disc_summ.jsp?cntn_id=135498&org=NSF "what is visual proprioception?".

[37] http://nationalgeographic.co.id/berita/2015/02/mampu-berdiri-satu-kaki-artinya-otak-sehat

[38] http://www.suaramerdeka.com/harian/0410/25/ragam05.htm

[39] http://intisari.grid.id/Wellness/Psychology/Membaca-Sifat-Manusia-Dari-Empat-Emosi-Dasar

[40] Nurdiansyah, Nia.,"Buku Pintar Ibu & Bayi". Bukune, 2011, hlm. 258.

[41] https://en.wikipedia.org/wiki/Amygdala

[42] https://en.wikipedia.org/wiki/Hippocampus

[43] https://id.wikipedia.org/wiki/Persepsi

[44] https://en.wikipedia.org/wiki/Fight-or-flight_response#Reaction

[45] C. Crochemore, J. Lu, Y. Wu, Z. Liposits, N. Sousa, F. Holsboer, O. F. X. Almeida.,

"Direct targeting of hippocampal neurons for apoptosis by glucocorticoids is reversible by mineralocorticoid
   receptor activation". Molecular Psychiatry (2005) 10, 790–798. doi:10.1038/sj.mp.4001679; published online
   17 May 2005. http://www.nature.com/mp/journal/v10/n8/full/4001679a.html?foxtrotcallback=true

[46] https://en.wikipedia.org/wiki/Cortisol#Memory

[47] McGaugh. J, Cahil. L, Roozendal. B, (1996) Involvement of the amygdala in memory storage: Interaction with
   other brain Systems. Proceedings of the National Academy of Sciences of the United States of America Vol.
   93, pp. 13508–13514, November 1996 f

[48] Ibid

[49] Conners, Kevin., "Help, My body Is Killing Me! (Stress and Autoimmune Disorders)". http://www.connersclinic.com/wp-content/uploads/2015/09/Help-Book-Section-2-PDF.pdf

[50] https://en.wikipedia.org/wiki/Effects_of_stress_on_memory#Short-term_memory

[51] "Anxiety and Peeing Problems". https://www.calmclinic.com/anxiety/signs/peeing-problems

[52] Hall, Calvin.S., Lindzey, Gardner.,"Teori-Teori Psikodinamik (Klinis)". Kanisius, 1993, hlm. 89.

[53] Anindyaputri, Irene.," Mengapa Orang Bisa Ketakutan Sampai Pingsan?". https://hellosehat.com/hidup-
   sehat/fakta-unik/pingsan-karena-ketakutan/

[54] https://en.wikipedia.org/wiki/Amygdala_hijack

[55] https://id.wikipedia.org/wiki/Dopamin

[56] BBC., "UK soldier and veteran suicides 'outstrip Afghan deaths'". http://www.bbc.com/news/uk-23259865

[57] https://id.wikipedia.org/wiki/Abraham_Maslow

[58] https://m.tempo.co/read/news/2016/07/22/103789769/nasib-rio-haryanto-di-f1-tak-jelas-menpora-minta-
   maaf

[59] https://www.merdeka.com/peristiwa/perjuangan-rio-haryanto-kandas-setengah-musim-di-laga-f1.html

[60] https://tirto.id/asian-games-1962-dan-politik-mercusuar-bung-karno-cS69

[61] "Nominasi Grammy Awards ke-59, Joey Alexander Masuk Nominasi Best Improvised Jazz Solo".
   https://hot.detik.com/grammy2017/music/d-3364589/joey-alexander-masuk-nominasi-best-improvised-

jazz-solo.

[62] https://en.wikipedia.org/wiki/Bill_Gates "Early life".

[63] https://en.wikipedia.org/wiki/Mark_Zuckerberg "College years".

[64] https://en.wikipedia.org/wiki/Bill_Gates "Early life".

[65] https://en.wikipedia.org/wiki/Sigmund_Freud#Dreams "Dreams".

[66] http://www.why-we-dream.com/schizresearch.htm

[67] http://health.kompas.com/read/2011/05/05/16233295/Berkepribadian.Labil.Sasaran.Cuci.Otak

[68] https://en.wikipedia.org/wiki/Lucy_(2014_film)#Critical_reception

[69] http://www.imdb.com/title/tt2872732/quotes

[70] https://m.tempo.co/read/news/2016/02/04/078742276/teroris-jual-janji-bidadari-di-surga-ini-antisipasi-luhut

[71] Chopra, Deepak., "Buddha". PT. Gramedia Jakarta, 2008

[72] https://id.wikipedia.org/wiki/Siddhartha_Gautama#Kelahiran

[73] Chopra, Deepak., "Buddha". PT. Gramedia Jakarta, 2008, hlm. 52

[74] Guruge, W.P. Ananda., "Mara Si Penggoda". Insight, 2014

[75] Chopra, Deepak., "Buddha". PT. Gramedia Jakarta, 2008, hlm. 198-202

[76] Ibid., hlm. 303-304

[77] Ibid., hlm. 309-320

[78] Ibid., hlm. 320-324

[79] Ibid., hlm. 325-327.

[80] Silananda, Sayadaw, U., "Meditasi Jalan". https://samaggi-phala.or.id/naskah-dhamma/meditasi-jalan/

[81] "Trisila kejawen : Menguak misteri dari ojo dumeh, eling lan waspodo". http://bpad.jogjaprov.go.id/coe/article/trisila-kejawen-menguak-misteri-dari-ojo-dumeh-eling-lan-waspodo-761

[82] https://www.kompas.com/tren/read/2020/03/24/221811865/tentang-serat-kalatidha-ronggowarsito-yang-dikutip-hb-x-saat-sapa-aruh-soal?page=all

[83] Lorenz, Konrad., "On Aggresion". The Taylor and Francis e-Library, 2005, hlm. 228.

[84] https://sejarawan.wordpress.com/2008/06/19/runtuhnya-romawi-dan-berkembangnya-agama-nasrani/ "D. Berkembangnya Agama Nasrani"

[85] Ibid

[86] "Witch-hunt". https://en.wikipedia.org/wiki/Witch-hunt

[87] http://www.katolisitas.org/penjualan-surat-pengampunan-dosa-di-abad-pertengahan/

[88] https://id.wikipedia.org/wiki/Perang_Salib "Perang Salib".

[89] https://id.wikipedia.org/wiki/Kerajaan_Champa

[90] https://id.wikipedia.org/wiki/Galileo_Galilei

[91] "Depresi Besar Dunia 'Malaise' (1929-1939)". http://www.hariansejarah.id/2017/04/depresi-besar-dunia-malaise-1929-1939.html

[92] "Fiat money". https://en.wikipedia.org/wiki/Fiat_money#20th_century

[93] Berger A.A. (2016) A Psychoanalytic Approach to Marketing. In: Marketing and American Consumer Culture. Palgrave Macmillan, Cham.

[94] http://www.psychologymania.com/2012/06/pengertian-perilaku-konsumtif.html

[95] http://www.radar-karawang.com/2016/10/pr-dihapus-tahun-depan.html?showComment=1477057215255

[96] http://news.metrotvnews.com/read/2015/05/19/127343/un-sd-dihapus-ini-yang-menjadi-penentu-kelulusan

[97] http://www.antaranews.com/berita/505660/jokowi-tempatkan-ekonomi-kerakyatan-sebagai-pilar-penting-bangsa

ABOUT THE AUTHOR

Bayu Jatmiko

Bayu Jatmiko is an Independent Scientist in the field of Psychology, holding a Bachelor's degree in Psychology, with a research focus on emotions and basic instincts. His journey started from his  curiosity during his orientation program in the Mechanical Engineering Faculty at a state university in East Java, Indonesia. There, he felt a sense of unease due to fear when senior students displayed aggressive behavior. He wondered, "Why are my seniors trying to frighten me while also asking me to think? How can I think when I'm feeling afraid?" From this point, his desire to explore human emotions grew, leading him to switch to the Faculty of Psychology, and eventually becoming an author and an independent researcher in the field of emotions and basic instincts.

Email : bayujatmiko@yahoo.com

www.ingramcontent.com/pod-product-compliance
Lightning Source LLC
Chambersburg PA
CBHW050814260726
48660CB00004B/1429